THE REASONS OF THE HEART

THE
REASONS OF
THE HEART

*A Journey into Solitude and Back
Again into the Human Circle*

JOHN S. DUNNE

Macmillan Publishing Co., Inc.
NEW YORK

Collier Macmillan Publishers
LONDON

Macmillan Publishing Co., Inc.
866 Third Avenue, New York, N.Y. 10022
Collier Macmillan Canada, Ltd.

Library of Congress Cataloging in Publication Data

Dunne, John S   1929–
    The reasons of the heart.

    1. Solitude—Addresses, essays, lectures. 2. God
—Addresses, essays, lectures. 3. Life—Addresses, es-
says, lectures. I. Title.
BJ1499.S6D86   248   77–16082
ISBN 0–02–533950–8

FIRST PRINTING 1978

Printed in the United States of America

Contents

Preface

THERE is a dilemma that arises whenever one chooses a road in life. It is that of "the road not taken."[1] If I give my life to something, then I have not given it to something else; if I share my life with someone, then I have not shared it with someone else. No matter what road I take, there will be a loss: there will be a road—in fact, many roads—I have not taken.

Is there a road in life I can follow with all my heart? Is there a path of heart's desire? If there is always a loss, always a road not taken, it may seem the human heart will always be divided. I will always be divided between something and something else, between someone and someone else. If there is a heart's desire, on the other hand, there may be a road leading to its fulfillment. I may be able to give my life to something, to share my life with someone. What is the heart's desire? If I let myself feel the loss of the road not taken, if I let myself feel the loneliness of the road I have taken, I am led on a journey into my heart, I come to know my heart's desire, and not only my own but that of others as well; I am led on a journey into the human heart.

That is the journey I wish to describe in this book. I invite my readers to come with me on a journey into the human heart. We will be going on an adventure of the mind that will also be an adventure of the heart.

Our starting point will be the loneliness of the human condition, the loneliness that is felt when one is choosing a road in life, that is felt in all the boundary situations of life: circumstance and conflict and suffering and guilt and death. It is a loneliness that is not taken away even when human beings are close to one another. There is a longing in that loneliness. It is the longing that I will call "the heart's desire." To come to know the human heart, it seems, we must go out to meet our loneliness in solitude, and then we must come back again to meet it in the human circle. So our journey into the human heart will be a withdrawal and a return, a journey "there and back again," as in fairy tales, a journey into solitude and back again into the human circle.

"Take the pupil of possibility, set him in the midst of the Jutland heath where nothing happens, where the greatest event is that a partridge flies up noisily," Kierkegaard says, "and he experiences everything more perfectly, more precisely, more profoundly, than the man who was applauded upon the stage of universal history, in case he was not educated by possibility."[2]

That is how I propose to begin—by going out into solitude "where nothing happens," hoping there to experience things "more perfectly, more precisely, more profoundly." What can we expect to learn in solitude? "Possibility," Kierkegaard says, the many possible roads we can take in life, but above all, we can say, the possibility of fulfilling the heart's desire. When we are alone, it is our loneliness, the longing in our loneliness, our heart's desire, that we experience "more perfectly, more precisely, more profoundly." In fact, we can expect our heart's desire to kindle in solitude, and when it has kindled, to illumine all the roads of life. We can expect to find "the way of possibility,"[3] as Dag Hammarskjöld calls it, the path of heart's desire.

If we are actually to travel the way, though, if we are to learn from actuality as well as from possibility, then it seems we must come back again into the human circle. Actuality, as it turns out, may not be simply the realization of possibility. Instead of a simple fulfillment of heart's desire there may be a finding and a losing, and then a losing and a finding, as in the saying of Jesus, "He who finds his life will lose it, and he who loses his life for my sake will find it."[4] Dante, for instance, found "a new life"[5] when he found Beatrice and lost it when he lost her in death; but then he found it and her again by somehow passing through death himself while he was still alive. Kierkegaard, on the other hand, found Regina and lost her in estrangement, but then he failed to find her again and succeeded only in coming to himself.

What do we come to if we follow the path of heart's desire? Ourselves or something greater than ourselves? That is our question. The journey of the human spirit, we can say with Hegel, is a journey in which we come to ourselves. The ultimate society, we can say with Marx, is a society in which we come to ourselves. It is by coming to ourselves, we can say with Kierkegaard, that we come to God. Yet it seems we can come in actuality to something greater than ourselves. We can come to be caught up like Dante in "the love that moves the sun and the other stars."[6]

Our myth, the prevailing story in our times, it seems, is the story of the self. It makes it difficult for us to see beyond selfhood. "Do you want to know what is lacking in you?", Al-Alawi once said to Marcel Carret. "To be one of us and to see the Truth, you lack the desire to raise your Spirit above yourself. And that is irremediable."[7] That is the difficulty we have with all the great religions, not only with Sufism and its way of raising one's Spirit above oneself or with Buddhism and its way of "no self" (*anatta*),[8] but also with Christianity, where we have learned our esteem for selfhood. We "lack the desire" in that our heart's desire is only a weak longing, a pining, a languishing, until our heart is kindled with the excitement of walking the path of heart's desire.

Let us be guided by Christianity on our journey into the human heart, hoping to discover the path of heart's desire, hoping to emerge from the story of self. I am calling the book *The Reasons of the Heart*, thinking of Pascal's saying, "The heart has its reasons that reason does not know."[9] Pascal was thinking especially, it seems, of the reasons of the heart at work in Christian believing. Those are the ones we too must consider. What are the reasons of the heart at work in Christian believing? Although "reason does not know" them, they can become known to the mind. It is when the reasons of the heart become known to the mind, I believe, that insight occurs. There is method in this, a method that can serve on our journey. At every turning point in our journey, we can hope, reasons of the heart will come to light. It is true, we will be coming upon an unfulfilled heart's desire everywhere we turn. Still, the way we are following, into solitude and back again into the human circle, may itself be the path leading to fulfillment. We may be entering already upon the path of heart's desire, taking our first steps on it, when we enter upon our journey into the heart.

I gave the essence of the following chapters as Sarum Lectures at Oxford in the Fall of 1976. I have added "A Note on Method," a note on my method in this and previous books, relating method to the story of self, to "I am" and "I will die," that is, to passing over to others and coming back to self, and to the spiritual adventure that carries us beyond ourselves. I would like to thank my friends at Oxford for the warm reception they gave me and for the kind hospitality they showed me, and to thank especially Dennis Nineham and Maurice Wiles for the encouragment they gave me while I was giving the lectures.

THE REASONS OF THE HEART

1

A Solitary Man's Journey

ONCE during his adventures in the desert, when he was bathing in a spring among the rocks, T. E. Lawrence saw approaching him "a grey-bearded, ragged man, with a hewn face of great power and weariness." The old man came up to the spring and, after looking at Lawrence for a moment, closed his eyes and groaned, "The love is from God and of God and towards God."[1]

The old man was a devastated human being, "moaning strange things, not knowing day and night, not troubling himself for food or work or shelter."[2] Yet he had that "hewn face of great power and weariness" and he uttered that great sentence about the to-and-fro between man and God. There is a common notion of God according to which whatever happens is the "will of God," and whatever happens beyond human control, such as a flood or a storm or an earthquake, is an "act of God," and an afflicted person like this old man is a "child of God." That God is a God of calamities. The old man himself, though, speaking from within affliction, sees God differently; sees a love coming from God into man and going back from man to God. His experience, if we can suppose that he experienced the love of which he spoke, places him among God's friends.

We have a choice, if we wish to know God, between learning from the friends of God and learning from the common notion. I would choose to learn from the friends of God. The common notion is a way of interpreting whatever happens, but it does not seem to arise out of any actual communication between God and man. The friends of God, on the contrary, walk and speak with God, experience a love that is "from God and of God and towards God." The to-and-fro with God in which they live seems to be the only real knowing of God that man has reached. To actually know God ourselves we will have to enter ourselves into the to-and-fro. Maybe from that vantage point we may be able to see the common notion in a new light. It too has to do with experiences: floods, storms, earthquakes, afflictions, and in fact everything that happens whatsoever. If we trace the journey of the friends of God, if we follow them to and from God, we may find ourselves following the to-and-fro with God through the region of all these other experiences, following, for instance, the love the old man speaks of through the region of the affliction he suffers.

I. THE ROAD TO GOD

After hearing the old man's words about the to-and-fro between God and man, Lawrence brought him to his camp and gave him supper, hoping for some further utterance. But the old man would say nothing. Later he rose up and wandered off into the night, withdrawing again into his solitude. His access to God was perhaps the solitude in which he lived. There is an African love song that consists of a single sentence:

I walk alone.[3]

Love, according to the song, is loneliness, and loneliness is love, a longing for communion with another. There is a depth of loneliness that remains untouched, though, even when one is communing with another human being. That loneliness can become love too, can become a longing for communion with God. When one lives down in that loneliness, as the old man apparently did, one is living in a solitude that is inaccessible to other human beings. There is the danger that one will never come up into the solitude that other persons can touch. That, it seems, was the old man's affliction: he never communicated with others, "never replied a word, or talked aloud, except when abroad by himself or alone among the sheep and goats."[4]

Deep solitude is a journey's end. It is the end of a journey inward to the source of one's being, a long and dangerous journey into the self and beyond the self. The ultimate danger is to become unable to return like the old man Lawrence met. The old man seems to stand at the end of withdrawal and the beginning of return, but not to have entered upon the return except for the brief moment when he spoke to Lawrence. The more immediate danger, especially for the modern man, is that one will feel cut off in that deep solitude, not only from human beings, but from God; that one will have journeyed into the self but be unable to get beyond the self. The old man could feel in touch with God, since for him "the love is from God" and not just "towards God." For him there is a to-and-fro. If one were to have no sense of a to-and-fro but only of a "to," only of a solitude and a longing, then one would feel cut off from God. One would find oneself in the position of K., the main character in Kafka's unfinished novel *The Castle*, always striving to gain access to the castle and never succeeding. God would appear to one much as the Castle appeared to K.— inaccessible.

Let us imagine a man setting out on a journey to the source of his being and encountering these dangers. Let us imagine him encountering first the more immediate danger of becoming trapped in the self. Then let us imagine him going on to encounter the more ultimate danger of becoming stranded beyond the self. Let us see what it would take to pass through these dangers.

He sets out, let us say, with high hopes of finding the source of his being, as though it were like a well at the world's end from which he could drink and be cured of all sorrow. There are three forms of perfect happiness on earth, Isak Dinesen says in her *Last Tales*. One is "to feel in oneself an excess of strength"; another is "to know for certain that you are fulfilling the will of God"; and the third is "the cessation of pain."[5] The man we are imagining has hopes of finding all three of these if he can find within himself the source of his being. That source would be an inexhaustible source of strength; it would be God; and to have God's companionship would take away the pain of his aloneness. As it is, he has no inner source of strength other than his hope of finding one. It is his hope that sustains him. Yet it sustains him well. As hope rises in him, life rises, and he seems to radiate an excess of life, almost as if he had already found the source and were living out of it.

His notion of God before this hope arose in him was simply the common notion. When he thought of fulfilling the will of God, he was thinking of the common notion that whatever happens is the will of God. To be happy, he thought, was to be in agreement with what is happening, to be in agreement with the human condition and with his own condition in life.[6] His happiness now, though, is in having found his quest, his inward journey to the source of his being. He expects now to come upon something that will change his life and make him a new man. In fact, the anticipation of it is already doing that, his life is already changing, a new man is already emerging. Before he found his adventure, he felt lost and aimless. There seemed to be nothing to do, nowhere to go. Now that he has found it, he has something to live for. The thought occurs to him that the inward journey is the will of God for him, that following it out means fulfilling God's will. That thought carries him some distance beyond the common notion. God's will is no longer simply what happens to him. It is rather an adventure that he is to undertake.

When he was trying to live in accord with his condition in life, he was trying to overcome the pain of his aloneness by becoming willing to walk alone. It was his unwillingness, he thought, that made his aloneness painful. If he could only become willing to walk alone, he could be alone and happy. Now that he has started his quest for the source of his being, he sees his aloneness as a longing for communion with God. To consent to aloneness now means for him to be willing to long for communion. It means to enter upon the adventure and go in search of God. Now he is alone and happy. He walks alone on his adventure. He is willing to go alone on his quest. But he lives in the prospect of being unalone. His happy aloneness is the other side of an aloneness that is still unhappy.

It is at this point that he encounters the first great peril of his journey, that of becoming trapped in the self. Whenever the unhappy aloneness becomes uppermost in his mind, he feels cut off from God and from other human beings. He is like Kafka writing "There is no one here who has an understanding for me in full [*im ganzen*]. To have even one who had this understanding, for instance a woman, would be to have support from every side. It would be to have God."[7] That suggests the need for intimacy with other human beings is a need to be understood by them, to be understood by at least one. To be understood, moreover, would be to have God; that is, it would be to have the happiness one looks for from the source of one's being. There would be that feeling of strength in oneself, though it would be coming from another person rather than from an inner source. There would also be that sense of accord with God, implicit in the accord and sympathetic understanding one would be receiving from the other. There would even be relief from the pain of aloneness insofar as understanding could reach to the deep aloneness that is not touched in other forms of intimacy.

To be understood in this way, however, may not be possible without first becoming luminous on that deep level by carrying through one's inward journey to the source of one's being. When one is in the midst of the journey, as is the man we are imagining, one is still dark on that level. The understanding he is seeking may be the kind one finds on the return journey from the source back into the self and on to others. He is caught, it seems, between the desire to go inward to the source and the desire to be understood by another, between the inward journey and the equal and opposite journey of return. If he does not choose between them, he will remain suspended between God and the other, suspended in the middle that is the self. If he chooses to search for understanding from another human being, there is the likelihood that he will fail to find it, since he is still dark on the level of his deep aloneness. The only way to emerge from the self, it appears, is to take the road of the inward journey.

He finds it difficult to trust the spiritual adventure to carry him there and back again, there to the source and back again to intimacy with others. It seems too spiritual, too inward. And at this point it is moving away from the understanding of others. But now that he has entered into his own solitude and experienced his own aloneness, it seems to be the way, and the only way. So he chooses to trust it, let us say. He gives himself over to it. He decides to rely on it, however one-sided it seems to be, to bring him into touch with God and with himself and with others, to make him a whole man.

As soon as he gives himself over to the spiritual adventure, he begins to be caught up in and carried by it. The deep loneliness he has felt begins to change from an ineffectual to a powerful longing. It changes from a languishing into a love, into "the love" the old man spoke of to Lawrence. The difference between the love the old man experienced and the deep loneliness anyone can experience seems to lie in this: not everyone gives himself over to the loneliness and the longing, not everyone stakes his life on the spiritual adventure that arises out of it. When someone does stake his life on it, then the languishing becomes the love. It ceases to be ineffectual and becomes powerful. To experience it in this powerful state is "to feel in oneself an excess of strength," a strength to bear one's life, a strength to live one's life to the full.

When the languishing becomes "the love," one seems to get caught up in the mighty circulation the old man spoke of that is "from God and of God and towards God." It is like the circulation of the blood and God is like the heart. The languishing is like the exhausted blood that flows through the veins to the heart to be renewed, and the love is like the renewed blood that flows from the heart through the arteries back into the body. The discovery of God takes place when the languishing becomes the love, when the power of the love is felt, when the exhausted life is renewed in the heart. The man we have been imagining has already passed from the common notion of God to that of a God who leads one on the spiritual adventure. Now as he becomes caught up in the adventure, he discovers its circular path. He discovers the to-and-fro of man with God. The will of God, as he sees it now, is the to-and-fro. To enter into the great circulation of love, to let oneself be carried by the love, is to let oneself be led by God, it is "to know for certain that you are fulfilling the will of God."

The only form of happiness that still seems denied to him is "the cessation of pain." He still feels the pain of his aloneness. The love sustains him but it does not satisfy his desires; it feeds mind and heart but it leaves them with their own hunger and thirst. The sense of being carried by the love, of being led by it, is a sense of living in touch with God, of walking with God, but he still has a sense also of walking alone. Maybe, he reflects, it is the lack of human companionship. Maybe it is simply the need to let the renewed life flow through the arteries and back into the body, the need to return to himself and to others.

2. THE ROAD FROM GOD TO GOD

Here he meets the second great peril of his adventure, that of becoming stranded in deep solitude and being unable to return. Although the love does not take away the pain of aloneness, although it is sustaining rather than satisfying, he finds that its power to sustain seems to increase as he relies on it alone and does not seek any other form of sustenance. The love is the excitement of the spiritual adventure, and the more he gives himself over to the adventure the more he feels the excitement and the more he is caught up in it and carried by it. The excitement is that of understanding and loving, not yet that of being understood and being loved. If he were to turn toward being understood and being loved, if he were to go back to others, he fears, the fire of understanding and loving would begin to die in him. "To be loved means to be consumed," Rilke says, "to love is to give light with inexhaustible oil. To be loved is to pass away, to love is to endure."[8] As long as he lives in the excitement of understanding and loving, he will give light with inexhaustible oil, he will endure. If he once turns toward being understood and being loved, he fears, he will begin to be consumed, he will begin to pass away.

If he follows the circulation of the love out from God into himself and into others, he foresees, its strength may gradually diminish, just like the blood that flows through the arteries into the body, until it becomes once more the languishing and flows back toward God, like the exhausted blood that flows back through the veins to the heart. If, on the other hand, he stays with the source of his being and draws upon it alone for his sustenance, the love will grow stronger and stronger and the sense of walking with God will become more and more vivid until perhaps it even takes away the pain of his aloneness. The circulation of the love, it is true, is not a natural process like the circulation of the blood. The love will become the languishing only if he seeks to be understood and loved and does not find what he is seeking. If, on the other hand, he does not seek anything from others but is content to understand and to love, then he cannot be disappointed. What the circulation of the love is calling for, it seems, is that he take the risk of being disappointed, that he let himself be carried by the love into communication with others, seeking to be understood by them, seeking to share the love with them.

He decides to give himself over to the circulation of love, let us say, and see where it leads him. It will lead him from God to others, he knows, but it remains to be seen whether the love will become once more the languishing before it leads him back to God. He meditates on figures who seem to embody the circulation of love, especially the figure of Jesus in the Gospel of John who speaks again and again of coming "from God" and going "to God."[9] If one were to give oneself over to "the love" the old man spoke of, then one's whole life would be "from God and of God and towards God," and if one were to

come back among others, instead of remaining in solitude as
the old man did, one might even begin to speak as Jesus does
in the Gospel of John or as the old man himself did when he
broke his silence for that one moment.

No doubt it is one thing to say what the old man said of "the
love" and another to say it, as Jesus did, of oneself. If the love
were to become one's whole life, it would become nearly possible to speak that way. For then the love would become like
"the life," and when one began to speak of it and communicate
it to others, it would become like "the light" in the Gospel of
John. But even then the love would still be something one was
caught up in, something larger than oneself. The man we are
imagining, since he has had to choose once and again to give
himself over to the love, is well aware that he himself is not the
love. Thus he is able to make all the statements of John's
Gospel, but of the love and not of himself. Where Jesus says "I
am,"[10] he must say "It is." Where Jesus says "I am the life"
and "I am the light," he must say "It is the life" and "It is the
light." Where Jesus says "I come from God," and "I go to
God," he must say "It comes from God" and "It goes to God."

There is a danger, he can see, of erasing the line between
God and the self, and there is a further danger, as he goes on
to commune with other persons, of erasing the line between
the self and others. "I in them, and thou in me"[11] is the formula Jesus used in the Gospel of John, "I in them" apparently
erasing the line between the self and others, and "thou in me"
apparently erasing the line between God and the self. "It is the
love," our solitary man must say, "that is in God and in me
and in others."

Yet there are figures who give themselves over to the love
and who do come to speak like Jesus in the Gospel of John.
There is Al-Hallaj, who met a death like that of Jesus on the
scaffold for saying, like Jesus, "I am the Truth."[12] His last

words were an expression of the love, "The ecstatic wants only to be alone with his Only One."[13] And there is Sri Ramakrishna who said, thinking of himself and of previous figures who embodied the love, "If you see a man endowed with ecstatic love, overflowing with ardor, mad after God, intoxicated with this love, then know for certain that God has incarnated himself through that man."[14] It is the mark of such figures that their love is "ecstatic," that they are so caught up in the love that they are beside themselves or outside themselves. Thus the line between God and the self tends to vanish. And so also does the line between the self and others. The man we have been imagining falls short of such figures. Still he is caught up in the love, caught up in the excitement of the spiritual adventure. There are degrees of being caught up, it seems, degrees of ecstasy, and they approach a limit situation, just as the curve of an hyperbola as it is carried out farther and farther approaches the line of the asymptote. The limit situation, the asymptote, would be the one described in the Gospel of John where it becomes true to say, "I am" rather than "It is," where it becomes true to say, "I in them, and thou in me."

"I am" and "It is" each tell a story. "Within our whole universe," Dinesen says in her *Last Tales*, "the story only has authority to answer that cry of heart of its characters, that one cry of heart of each of them: 'Who am I?' "[15] Jesus can say "I am" in the Gospel of John because his story is the story of the love that comes from God and goes to God. "I came from the Father, and have come into the world," he tells his disciples in his last discourse, "and again, I am leaving the world, and going to the Father."[16] That sentence appears to tell the whole story as it is understood in the Gospel of John. Its importance comes out in the way the disciples respond to it, "Ah, now you are speaking plainly, not in any figure!"[17]

If the man we are imagining were to ask himself "Who am I?", he would have to tell the story we have been telling, how he has passed from the loneliness to the love. Thus his story would not be simply that of the love. It would be first of all that of the loneliness. He enters into the story of the love when the ineffectual longing becomes powerful, when he enters upon the spiritual adventure. Actually a person's story can be told in different ways, with different degrees of inwardness, the most inward being that of the spiritual adventure. In its least inward form it is the story of what happens to him, of the things and situations of his life. In a somewhat more inward form it is the story of what he does, more inward because then it is essentially the story of the choices he makes, how he relates to things and situations. In a still more inward form it is the story of what he says, or better, of what he has to say, the story of his message, of what he has to communicate to others, his insight into his experience. In its most inward form, as that of a spiritual adventure, it is the story of the meaning he embodies in his life and death, the story of what he incarnates.

Telling the story of what has happened to him, our solitary man would have to tell how in pursuing the fulfillment of his deepest needs, his longing for communion on the deepest level of his life, he has let his other needs, especially his longing for simple human intimacy, go unfulfilled. His situation is the reverse of what happens to someone who is suffocating in human intimacy for lack of solitude. He is hungering and thirsting in solitude for lack of human intercourse. This unfulfillment of simple human needs may be part of what he is experiencing when he finds the love that comes from God and goes to God sustaining but not satisfying. It may be part also of what is leading him now to return to other human beings and not simply remain alone with God. His story seems to contrast on this matter of unfulfillment with the one being told in the Gospel of John. "Whoever drinks of the water that I shall give him will never thirst," Jesus tells the woman at the well, "but the water that I shall give him will become in him a spring of water welling up to eternal life."[18]

It may be that the water of the inner well is meant only to satisfy spiritual needs, to fulfill the deep longing of the human spirit for God, and not to satisfy simple human needs or to fulfill the simple human longing for other human beings. "It seems to be difficult for the individual to realize that there exists a division between one's spiritual and purely human needs," Otto Rank says, "and that the satisfaction or fulfilment for each has to be found in different spheres."[19] Rank is thinking, however, of someone who tries to fulfill his spiritual needs through human relationships. What of someone, like our solitary man, who has done the opposite, who has gone into solitude to find the source of his being?

There is a clue in the Gospel of John in the saying of Jesus, "I have food to eat which you do not know"—the metaphor has changed from drink to food—"My food is to do the will of him who sent me, and to accomplish his work."[20] There is a sense here of relating to other human beings out of a fullness rather than an emptiness. It may be that the division between spiritual and purely human needs, as Rank understands it, reflects a state of emptiness, the state of languishing in which one experiences a loneliness that is not touched in human intercourse. As one passes from the languishing to the love it becomes possible to relate to others out of a fullness. The will of God is no longer what happens to one but is something to be done, as in this saying of Jesus, something to be accomplished. Thus one passes from the story of what happens to one to the story of what one does. Doing the will of God, it seems, means sharing the love with others, relating to them out of the fullness of the love rather than out of the emptiness of the languishing. One is nourished and sustained then by that fullness itself, by what one has to communicate. As one goes inward thus from what happens to one to what one does to what one has to communicate, one seems to go from an unfulfillment to a fullness. There would be only one further step inward and that would be, if one were able, to say that one is the sustenance, to tell the story as an incarnation of meaning, to say as Jesus does in the Gospel of John, "I am the bread of life."[21]

Here our solitary man comes to a halt upon "It is" and "I am." He cannot simply live in a fullness, he finds, but he has always to make a choice to relate to others out of a fullness rather than an emptiness. He has always to pass once more from emptiness to fullness. He cannot be an incarnation of the love but only of the movement from languishing to love. A formula for incarnation might be Shakespeare's saying:

> It hath been taught us from the primal state
> That he which is was wished until he were.[22]

A person embodies a longing. He is "wished until he were." A person who lives out his life in an emptiness and relates to others out of emptiness rather than fullness embodies human longing in the form of a languishing. The figure of Jesus in the Gospel of John embodies a love that comes from God and goes to God. Our solitary man embodies a passing from emptiness to fullness, a passing from languishing to love. In the language of the Gospel he embodies not "the life" so much as the "passing from death to life."[23]

God in our solitary man's vision, accordingly, is like God in the Gospel of John. He is implicitly defined by the "from and of and towards" and by "the love" that is "the life" and "the light." The will of God, instead of being simply whatever happens, is that human beings pass from languishing to love, that they pass from death to life, that they pass from darkness into light. The acts of God, instead of being events beyond human control such as floods and storms and earthquakes, are the communication of love to those who are languishing, of life to those who are dead, of light to those who are in darkness. And the children of God, instead of being those who are afflicted and who are outside the human circle, are those who pass from languishing to love, from death to life, from darkness into light.

But what about whatever happens? What about events beyond human control such as floods and storms and earthquakes? What about those who are afflicted and who are outside the human circle? These are questions our solitary man faces as he enters upon his return journey. He left them behind him on the inward journey when he left behind what Rank calls his "purely human needs," when he left behind the common notion of God and saw God as leading him forth on a spiritual adventure. Now the adventure itself brings him back to them. They may be linked to the condition he left behind when he passed from languishing to love. They have to do with the human condition, with human control, with the human circle. When he entered upon the spiritual adventure, the human condition changed for him from one of loneliness and ineffectual longing to one of love and adventure. He began to make choices then in the realm of the human condition, a realm ordinarily beyond the scope of human control and responsibility, first the choice to go through with the inward journey to the source of his being, then to make the journey of return to himself and to others. And now that he has entered upon the return journey, he faces the task of communicating with others in this realm, a realm of deep aloneness ordinarily outside the circle of human intercourse.

He has come upon great dangers in this realm, on the inward journey the danger of becoming trapped in the self and then of becoming stranded beyond the self, and now on the return journey he faces the danger of erasing the line between God and self and then between self and others. These lines have something to do with the human condition, the one between God and self with the limits of human control, and the one between self and others with the limits of the human circle. Maybe the greatest danger of the return, though, is to observe these lines between God and self and others so carefully, to keep within the human circle and the limits of human control so cautiously as to revert once more to the original human condition, to go back from the love to the languishing. Let us imagine our solitary man setting out on the return journey and meeting these dangers. Say he returns first to himself by letting his experience of the love become a vision of the mind and a vision of the heart. Then he returns to others by entering with this light into the darkness where human beings are ordinarily inaccessible to one another.

2

The Mind's Vision

"WHERE do you come from?" That is the question, Gnostic Christians believed, that is posed to the soul at death. If one has never entered into one's aloneness, it seems a simple question that asks about one's human origins. If one enters into one's aloneness, though, and finds there a life deeper than the life one draws from one's human connections, it seems a great question that looks to a source of life beyond the human circle. It goes with the other great question "Where are you going?"

To know would be Gnosis, spiritual knowledge. "He who possesses Gnosis," it is said in *The Gospel of Truth*, "knows where he comes from and where he is going."[1] We have found that, were we to ask the man we have been imagining, he would not be able to say, "I come from God" and "I go to God," like Jesus in the Gospel of John, speaking of the love that comes from God and goes to God. He would have to say, rather, "It comes from God" and "It goes to God." Thus, it seems, he would differ from a Gnostic. If he were to speak of the loneliness, however, that becomes the love, the deep loneliness that is to be found in every human being and that is a

longing and a languishing for God, he might be able to speak
of "I" rather than "It." For the loneliness is the heart of his
existence even before it is transformed into love. The old man
said to Lawrence, "The love is from God and of God and
towards God." Perhaps we could say, or have the man we are
imagining say, "The loneliness is from God and of God and
towards God." If he could rightly say that, then maybe he too
could say, "I come from God" and "I go to God."

There is a kind of knowing, Camus has shown, that comes
from living with the bare loneliness of the human condition. It
is the consciousness and lucidity of what he calls "the absurd
man":

What, in fact, is the absurd man? He who, without negating it,
does nothing for the eternal. Not that nostalgia is foreign to him.
But he prefers his courage and his reasoning. The first teaches him
to live without appeal and to get along with what he has; the
second informs him of his limits. Assured of his temporally limited
freedom, of his revolt devoid of future, and of his mortal consciousness, he lives out his adventure within the span of his
lifetime.[2]

Our solitary man, by contrast with the absurd man, does do
something for the eternal. He enters upon the spiritual adventure and his loneliness becomes love. The questions raised by
"nostalgia" are the essential ones for him: "Where do you
come from?" and "Where are you going?" Let us see what he
does, therefore, with what he has and with his limits. Let us see
with what vision he lives out his adventure.

1. "GOD IS HOW THINGS STAND"

"We shall treat first of God, second of the movement of the
rational creature towards God, third of Christ who as man is

the way for us of tending towards God."[3] That is the plan Aquinas outlines from his *Summa Theologiae*. It is a vision of the mind: all beings come from God, all human beings are called to return to God, and Christ is the way. A somewhat similar vision could arise from the experience of a loneliness that is "from God and of God and towards God." Our solitary man has entered through loneliness into the circulation of a love that comes from God and goes to God. He has been meditating, too, on the figure of Jesus in the Gospel of John, who comes from God and goes to God and seems thus to embody the circulation of the love. If he lets his experience of the spiritual adventure become a vision of the mind, it will take a form very similar to that of Aquinas, a great circle going from God to God with the figure of Jesus as the way.

Where his vision might differ from that of Aquinas is in his concept of the spiritual adventure. For Aquinas the spiritual adventure is "the movement of the rational creature towards God" and Christ is "the way for us of tending towards God." For the man we have been imagining, the spiritual adventure is more circuitous. It begins with an inward journey to God, the source of one's being. Then it goes full circle from God to God. And the figure of Jesus embodies the full circle. The larger circuit exists for Aquinas, too, but as a journey of the mind. First the mind goes on a journey to God by the "way of negation,"[4] coming to God by leaving behind all that is not God. Then it goes on a journey through the full circle from God to God by the "way of affirmation," following the path of God's own activity out from God and then following the path of human activity back to God. It is this human activity, the second half of the circle, that is "the movement of the rational creature towards God."

Now if the spiritual adventure were to go the whole circuit, as we have been envisioning, then the entire journey of the mind would take place along the path of the spiritual adventure. The way of negation would be along the path of the inward journey to God, and the way of affirmation would be along the path of the return journey from God to God. Let us imagine our solitary man making a journey of the mind, following with his mind the path of the spiritual adventure. Let us see if he would discover any more than someone making the journey simply as an adventure of the mind.

Let our starting point be the common notion of God, the notion that whatever happens is the "will of God," that whatever happens beyond human control is an "act of God," and that one who lives outside the human circle is a "child of God." The man we have been envisioning starts with this notion of God but is led beyond it by his experience of the spiritual adventure. The way of negation for him is essentially a *No* to the common notion, negating things ascribed to God in the common notion. But then he is led by the adventure itself back to the common notion or back to what the common notion is about, namely whatever happens, what is beyond human control, what is outside the human circle. As it turns out, the spiritual adventure does encompass whatever happens and does bring one into relationship with events, also with events beyond human control and with persons and regions within the person that are outside the human circle. So in the end our solitary man comes back to the common notion of God and finds a profound truth in it. The way of affirmation for him becomes a *Yes* to what the common notion is about, if not to the common notion itself, affirming that God's will does encompass whatever happens, that God's act does encompass what is beyond human control, that God is close to those who are outside the human circle.

When then is the meaning of the *No?* If there were no spiritual adventure, then we would be left with nothing but the common notion of God. We might be tempted to reduce God to what is in that notion, to conclude, like Wittgenstein in his *Notebooks*, "God is how things stand" and "How things stand is God."[5] What the spiritual adventure does—though it ultimately brings one back again—is to take one beyond "how things stand." It teaches one that "God is not how things stand" and "How things stand is not God." That is the first negation on the way of negation. Or it is the first, let us say, that our solitary man comes to. It amounts to saying that God is not domesticated by "how things stand," that God leads on an adventure, that God is wild.

"How things stand" includes the human condition, how things stand for us, the fact that we are always in situations, that we cannot live without conflict and suffering, that we cannot avoid guilt, that we must someday die, and that in all these things we are alone and cannot make one another unalone.[6] The spiritual adventure affects the aloneness by bringing one into touch with God and with oneself and with others. By reaching the aloneness it reaches everything else: circumstance, conflict, suffering, guilt, and death. Every facet of the human condition is transformed by it. So it becomes impossible for one who has entered upon it to regard his untransformed aloneness and death and guilt and suffering and conflict and circumstances as the "will of God," as in the common notion of God. He must say, "The will of God is not how things stand" and "How things stand is not the will of God." This is the second negation on the way of negation, and it is stronger than the first, for it is less to call "how things stand" the "will of God" than it is to call it "God," and so it is more to say *No* to the one than to the other. It amounts to saying that the will of God cannot be simply read off from facts or events but must be discerned, must be found through insight, through the kindling of the heart and the illumining of the mind that occur on the spiritual adventure.

A third and still stronger negation would be to say, "How things stand is not the act of God" and "The act of God is not how things stand." Here, though, the *No* may have gone too far. The question is whether the loneliness of the human condition is "from God and of God and towards God" or whether it becomes so only when it is transformed into "the love." When one says the human condition is not the will of God, one is saying the will of God is not fulfilled until the transformation takes place, until the loneliness becomes the love and the human condition is changed. If one goes on to say the human condition is not even the act of God, then one is saying the human condition is not "from God" until it is transformed. In reality, though, the loneliness of the human condition is a longing for communion with God, as our solitary man has experienced it, an ineffectual longing, to be sure, a pining and a languishing, but nevertheless a longing that is "towards God." It seems only a small step to say that it is also "from God."

God is at work, if that is true, in things as they stand, in the human condition, in death and guilt and suffering and conflict and all the situations of life. And to that extent the common notion of God is valid. Where our solitary man finds God, however, is not in the fact that these situations are beyond human control, as in the common notion, but in the loneliness for God that runs through them all. He sees already in the loneliness of the human condition the great circle going from God to God that appears in the love. He sees it also in the isolation of a person who is afflicted and who lives outside the realm of human intercourse. He is ready to agree with the common notion that an afflicted person is a "child of God." His *No* comes in the end to saying that all of these matters— "God," the "will of God," the "act of God," and the "child of God"—are revealed for what they are only when the loneliness of the human condition is transformed into love.

If our solitary man had lived his whole life in the love and had never lived, as a person in our times usually does, in the bare loneliness, then the way of negation would have been for him purely an adventure of the mind. He would have known the loneliness only as it appears in the mind itself, as the mind's longing to know God, what Aquinas calls the "natural desire"[7] of the mind to see God. And seeing how the longing is still unfulfilled, he would have concluded, like Aquinas, "We do not know what God is."[8] If, vice versa, he had lived his whole life in the loneliness of the human condition and had no experience of the love, then too the way of negation would have been for him purely an adventure of the mind. But, having no experience of being in touch with God, he would have concluded that God is "transcendent"[9] in Kant's meaning of the term, that God is beyond all human experience.

As it is, having the experience of living in the loneliness and then entering into the love, he has a sense of passing from an ignorance to a knowledge of God. He has a sense of coming to Gnosis, spiritual knowledge, knowing in the love the whence and whither of the loneliness. The passing from darkness to light, nevertheless, is still going on for him. In entering into the love, he realizes, he has not left the loneliness behind. Thus he differs from a Gnostic. He can agree that "It was this ignorance concerning the Father which produced anguish and terror," as it is said in *The Gospel of Truth*, but he cannot agree that the anguish and terror of the loneliness simply disappear for those who come to the light, that "if they attain to knowledge of the Father, oblivion becomes, at that very instant, non-existent," or that "deficiency, at that same instant, disappears."[10] For him the anguish and terror of the loneliness do not simply vanish but gradually give way to the love. He exists not in a high noon where there is no darkness but in a dawning where darkness is passing into light. He can there-

fore agree with Aquinas: "We do not know what God is." Yet
he can also say, "We are coming to know what God is." We are
learning what God is, insight by insight, according to his experience, as our loneliness is transformed into love.

There is a human experience of God, according to this, an
experience that is recognized in the love and that exists but
goes unrecognized in the loneliness. The act of recognizing it is
an insight into the experience, a knowing of its whence and
whither. The recognition occurs again and again, each time as
a new insight, as the transformation of loneliness into love
goes on. The anguish and terror of the loneliness appear again
and again, taking ever new forms. Each time our solitary man
meets them he has to come to terms anew with the "deficiency,"
the lack he experiences in the loneliness, and the "oblivion,"
the "ignorance" he finds there, that produce the anguish and
terror. Each time he has to see what the loneliness has to do
with God and what he must do to make the anguish and terror
give way to love. Each time he has to pass from a sense that
God is "transcendent" in Kant's meaning of the term, beyond
human experience, to a sense that God is "immanent," that his
experience is "from and of and towards" God.

As he goes from insight to insight, nevertheless, he realizes
that there is still a way in which God can be called "transcendent." It is not that God is beyond all human experience. It is,
rather, that the experience is inexhaustible, that further insight
is always possible. Here it makes sense for him to give his mind
over, like Aquinas or Spinoza, to the desire to know God, to
always seek that further insight. It is like giving his heart over,
as he has, to the love. It is a way of being a friend of God
where friendship reaches to the mind as well as the heart. Say
he does give his mind over, therefore, and does let it become
absorbed in the desire to know God. It points his mind towards
the life after death and the vision of God in the beyond, as one

might expect, but its immediate effect is to lead him back toward the human condition and its loneliness. For the desire to know God, as far as he can see, has its roots in the loneliness for God that pervades the human condition. In fact, it is that very loneliness, that very longing for God, as experienced in the mind. He proposes to follow his mind's desire, let us say, by following it to its roots. So he must turn around from the way of negation and travel back to common experience. He must travel the way of affirmation.

2. "GOD IS THAT ALL THINGS ARE POSSIBLE"

"What is laid upon us is to accomplish the negative," Kafka says, "the positive is already given."[11] That is the main difficulty our solitary man encounters as he travels the way of affirmation. He is coming back to the human condition, to what is "already given." There is little one can do with what is "already given," with the human condition, except fight it, surmount it, not succumb to it. "Life is denial,"[12] Kafka says. Our solitary man, nevertheless, has come to affirm it, to say *Yes* to it. He wants to find in the loneliness of the human condition the roots of "the love" and of the "natural desire" to see God. The situations that define the human condition, death and guilt and suffering and conflict and circumstance, he sees now, are the basic occasions of insight. No doubt, it is when the loneliness is transformed into love that insight occurs. Still he expects the insight to reach down into the loneliness itself.

What he is seeing now is like seeing how tragedy issues into insight, how a dramatist can take death and guilt and suffering and conflict and circumstance and make light come from their darkness. Only he sees how the situations themselves issue into insight even apart from the drama and even before the dramatist tries to make something of them. He sees death, his own death, as holding some ultimate insight for him. Every time he faces the prospect of death, let us say, he has a glimpse of it like an afterglow on the horizon. He sees the other situations, too, as holding some insight for him, guilt and suffering and conflict and circumstance. But the insight from these other situations always arises from going through and emerging from the darkness of the situations themselves, going through the experience of guilt by accepting responsibility for one's life and all its destructive consequences and emerging from it by forgiving and being forgiven, going through the experience of suffering by accepting the pain and the sense of loss and emerging from it by letting it purify the heart and make one heart-free, going through the experience of conflict by accepting the opposing forces within oneself and emerging from it by living out the struggle and letting the divided heart become a whole heart, going through the experience of situatedness by accepting the circumstances of one's life and emerging from it by coming to a new relationship with one's circumstances. With death, on the other hand, he has yet to go through and emerge; he can only go through the facing of death and emerge somehow from that into a new life that is still on this side of death.

It may be that the insight he senses hidden in death is the vision of God, as in the words of the Lord to Moses, "No man shall see me and live,"[13] as though to see God were death and death were to see God. At any rate, the will of God, as he sees things now, cannot be simply that we accept the situations of life but must be rather that we go through them and emerge from them. The acts of God likewise cannot consist simply in imposing the situations on life but must consist rather in leading us through them and out of them. The child of God too cannot be simply a person who is trapped in his affliction but must be rather one who is led by God to God through his affliction. Our solitary man's *Yes*, therefore, is not to death and guilt and suffering and conflict and circumstance but to going through them and emerging from them.

Yet not everyone goes through the situations of life and emerges from them. One may be unwilling to go through, unwilling to be in the situation one is in, to undergo the conflict, to suffer the pain and the loss, to take responsibility for the destructiveness of one's life, to die. Or one may be unwilling to emerge, unwilling to live in a new relationship with the circumstances of one's life, to become heart-whole, to become heart-free, to forgive and be forgiven, to come into a new life. So the will of God, as our solitary man now understands it, is not necessarily fulfilled, and the acts of God do not necessarily succeed. Everything depends on the *Yes* of the human being. There is a desire in the heart to go through and emerge, and there is a desire in the mind to come to the insight, but one doesn't necessarily consent either to the heart's desire or to the mind's desire.

If one consents to the mind's desire, giving the mind over to the desire to know God, like Aquinas or Spinoza, then the mind's longing is transformed into love. "The intellectual love of the mind towards God," Spinoza says, "is that very love of God whereby God loves himself."[14] That is like saying that the love of the mind is "from God and of God and towards God." If one consents to the mind's desire alone, however, without also consenting to the heart's desire, then it will not be at all apparent to one how a life on earth could be needful or even helpful toward attaining the mind's goal of seeing God. If one consents, first of all, to the heart's desire, like our solitary man, then it becomes apparent how the mind's insights arise out of the heart's adventures, how insight comes from going through the situations of life and emerging from them. Something like a vision of God, it appears then, would have to arise

from a whole lifetime of human experience, from going
through the situations of an entire life and emerging from them
in death. The vision of God would answer to the question that
runs through both the way of negation and the way of affirmation, "What is God?"

"God *is* that all things are possible," Kierkegaard says, "and
that all things are possible *is* God."[15] That, it seems, is what
one could say to the question "What is God?" at this point, not
having gone through the situations of an entire life and yet
being willing to go through. One is at the other end of the
journey from the experience formulated by Wittgenstein:
"God is how things stand" and "How things stand is God."
Both expressions are true to experience. "How things stand,"
though, describes the experience of one who has not yet entered upon the spiritual adventure, who knows only the loneliness of the human condition, how circumstance and conflict
and guilt and suffering and death all isolate one, how the more
intense one's taste or foretaste of them is, the more alone one is.

"All things are possible," on the other hand, describes the
experience of one who has entered upon the spiritual adventure, who knows what it is for the loneliness to become love.
When one looks at the circumstances of one's life, there is the
loneliness of knowing that one must live one's own particular
life, that one must take one's single way in life, which is one's
lot, one's portion. It is because the circumstances are inevitably particular. One has a way, but it is forced by the force of
circumstances. Let us call it the "way of necessity." When the
loneliness becomes love, on the other hand, the way is trans-
figured. It is the same way, but it is seen in the light of heart's
desire. Dag Hammarskjöld calls it the "way of possibility."[16]
The necessity was one of circumstances; the possibility is one
of heart's desire. It is the way on which one's heart's desire can
be fulfilled.

There is a conflict that comes to light, nevertheless, between one's heart's desire and one's circumstances, between what one wants to be and what one must be, between "all things are possible" and "how things stand." One may begin like Don Quixote by following one's heart's desire and end like Don Quixote on his deathbed by submitting to one's circumstances. Both ways are lonely ones, for if one follows heart's desire one is estranged from the circumstances of one's life, and if one submits to circumstances one is estranged from one's heart's desire. Either way one feels far removed from oneself. If one lives out the conflict, on the other hand, not choosing one over the other but holding fast to both heart's desire and circumstances, one can find whatever unity there is between what one wants to be and what one must be. Heart's desire and circumstances come together to define a path. The way of necessity and the way of possibility turn out to be one and the same way. "How things stand is that all things are possible," one can say, "and that all things are possible is how things stand."

Living out the conflict, though, means suffering the losses that circumstances impose upon heart's desire, suffering them without either giving up one's heart's desire or rejecting one's circumstances. The more intensely one feels the pain of loss the more alone one feels, just as all pain drives one into oneself, making it difficult to feel what others are feeling because one is so overwhelmed by what one is feeling. One may turn away from the loss and not let oneself feel the pain. Or one may be trapped in the pain and be unable to think of anything else. If the deep loneliness in one becomes love, on the other hand, one is able to dwell in the aloneness that pain causes without being destroyed by it. "Joy is deeper yet than agony,"[17] Nietzsche says. If the deep loneliness becomes love, then there is indeed a joy deeper than sorrow and, as the pain drives one into one's aloneness, one is able to go through the sorrow to the joy.

It is one's circumstances, if that is so, with all the loss they impose, that occasion the emergence of one's heart's desire. Still the pain of loss, while the emergence is coming about, can drive one to desperation, trying to fulfill heart's desire in spite of circumstances, or to despair, giving up heart's desire because of circumstances. In the desperation and the despair there is an element of ignorance, not understanding one's heart's desire, and an element of guilt, not waiting to understand it. "Because of impatience we were driven out," Kafka says, speaking of the sin that caused mankind to be driven out of paradise, "because of impatience we cannot return."[18]

Waiting to understand the heart's desire, one is waiting to become heart-free and heart-whole. One is waiting to be purified of desperation and despair. The waiting itself is already the beginning. If one continues to wait, one finds oneself going against a current of fear, the fear that leads back towards desperation and despair. It is fear that leads one to act in desperation, one realizes. It is fear that leads one to give up in despair. Fear of what? Of nothingness, Kierkegaard says.[19] Of death, we could say. The desperation and the despair arise when one's life opens up before one all the way to death. There is a loneliness one experiences in the face of death, the loneliness of having to die one's own death just as one has to live one's own life, the loneliness of having to live and die alone. It is the same deep loneliness, it seems, that we found at the core of human relationships. As the heart kindles, on the other hand, one enters into a love that "casts out fear." It is a love that casts out the fear leading to desperation and despair, the fear of death and nothingness. "There is no fear in love," it is said in the First Epistle of John, "but perfect love casts out fear."[20]

"Now is my soul troubled" even Jesus can say, even in the Gospel of John, when he is facing death. "Now shall the ruler of this world be cast out," he says, though, when he goes through fear to courage.[21] One goes through fear to courage, it seems, through desperation and despair to hope, through sorrow to joy, through conflict to peace, through circumstances to heart's desire. The way of necessity is the way of circumstance and conflict and suffering and guilt and death. The way of possibility is the way of "going through." "God is how things stand" for one who sees only the way of necessity. "God is that all things are possible" for one who sees the way of possibility. What is God, we can ask, for one who actually does "go through"?

3. "GOD IS SPIRIT"

"God is spirit,"[22] Jesus says in the Gospel of John, and that seems to intimate also the vision our solitary man is seeking. His experience takes place in the realm of the human spirit, the mind and the heart. It is the experience of a God who kindles his heart and illumines his mind, who leads him on a spiritual adventure. The term "spiritual" is defined by the adventure itself, by the course that it takes, and so is the term "spirit" and the saying "God is spirit" insofar as he can make the saying his own. The course the adventure takes is first away from the human condition and then back to the human condition. If we were to call the human condition "flesh," the meaning of "spirit" would at first be set against but then afterward would be found to encompass that of "flesh."

When the spiritual adventure is leading one beyond the human condition, from the loneliness and the languishing of the human condition to the love and the passion of the adventure, the meaning of "spirit" for one will be set over against that of "flesh." One's sense of it will be like that of Jesus in the Gospel of John, "It is the spirit that gives life, the flesh is of no avail."[23] But when the adventure is leading one back again to the human condition, back to find insight in the situations of human life, in circumstance and conflict and suffering and guilt and death, the meaning of "spirit" for one will somehow include that of "flesh." One's sense of it, then, will be like that in the prologue to the Gospel of John, "And the Word became flesh and dwelt among us."[24] The vision of God will seem hidden in the flesh of the human condition, and it will seem necessary to go through and emerge from the situations of human life to attain it.

When spirit is set over against flesh, it is experienced as a joy but a joy that does not take away pain. When it encompasses flesh, it is experienced as a fullness of joy that is reached by going through pain. At first joy is "to feel in oneself an excess of strength" and "to know for certain that you are fulfilling the will of God," but ultimately it becomes also "the cessation of pain."[25] Let us imagine our solitary man going through from the one kind of joy to the other. Let us see how flesh and spirit will change for him.

"These things I have spoken to you," Jesus says in the Gospel of John, "that my joy may be in you, and that your joy may be full."[26] When one enters upon the spiritual adventure, one enters into a joy that is the joy of the adventure itself. It makes one's life previous to the adventure seem sad by comparison. One never realized how unhappy one was until one experienced the joy of having found one's adventure, the joy of simply being on the adventure. The joy of the adventure, nevertheless, is not a fullness of joy. It is, rather, the experience of a desire that is still unfulfilled. Where before there was the sadness of a weak and ineffectual longing, there is now the exhilaration of a longing that has become powerful in the hope of fulfillment. But there is as yet no fulfillment. There is still the pain of unfulfillment, the pain of aloneness. The fullness of joy

would mean the fulfillment of the desire or, to put it nega-
tively, the cessation of the pain of aloneness. The words "that
my joy may be in you, and that your joy may be full" suggest
that a fullness of joy is indeed possible and that it comes about
when "my joy" is "in you."

Say our solitary man seeks to realize the truth of those
words "that my joy may be in you." The joy of Jesus, as it is
understood in the Gospel of John, seems to be the joy of being
who he is, of being the Son of God, of coming from God and
going to God. Our solitary man, too, has a sense of coming
from God and going to God, but it is more loneliness than joy.
It is felt as a pang of nostalgia. It becomes the great joy that is
"to feel in oneself an excess of strength" and "to know for
certain that you are fulfilling the will of God" only when he
enters upon the spiritual adventure, when he passes from the
story of the loneliness into that of the love. What he is realizing
now is that in entering into the story of the love, he is entering
into the relationship of Jesus with God.

As he seeks also to realize the truth of the words "and that
your joy may be full," however, he finds that his sharing in the
intimacy of Jesus with God is very incomplete. His joy is not
full. His experience of the spiritual adventure so far is one of
loving and understanding. What is missing is a sense of being
loved and being understood. It may be that this will come to
him only in actually going through the situations of his life:
going through guilt to a sense of forgiveness, through the inner
conflict of at once wanting and fearing to be understood and
loved, through the pain of aloneness at not being understood
and loved, through the sense of being unnecessary and un-
wanted, of being abandoned to die. In each instance he will be
going through pain to a "cessation of pain," not indeed to a
final cessation while he lives but to a cessation of pain in that
situation and thus to some taste of a fullness of joy.

Pain drives one into oneself, but joy carries one beyond oneself. The story of spirit as Hegel tells it in his *Phenomenology of Spirit*[27] is a story of coming to self, of man coming to himself or of God coming to himself in man. As we are telling it, on the other hand, it is a story of coming to joy, and thus of being carried beyond oneself. For Hegel spirit is selfhood; for us spirit is ecstasy. Still, it is by going through himself and the pain of his loneliness that our solitary man gets beyond himself to the joy of the love, and then it is by coming back through himself and the loneliness of the human condition that he comes to a fullness of joy. Standing in the middle ground of the self, spirit seems beyond him, as in the saying of Jesus, "The wind blows where it wills, and you hear the sound of it, but you do not know whence it comes or whither it goes."[28] Standing there in the self, and thinking of spirit as ecstasy, he can ask "whence it comes" and "whither it goes." Thinking of spirit as selfhood, he can ask himself the questions with which we began: "Where do you come from?" and "Where are you going?"

Both questions are posed to Jesus in the Gospel of John. Pilate asks him, "Where do you come from?" Peter asks him, "Where are you going?"[29] He keeps silence with Pilate. He speaks with Peter, but he says, "Where I am going you cannot follow me now, but you shall follow afterward." When he speaks directly to these questions, he speaks out of his selfhood, saying, "I come from God" and "I go to God." If our solitary man were to speak to these questions out of his selfhood, he would be speaking out of the nostalgia, the homesickness, the yearning for another condition that pervades human existence. When he faces circumstance and guilt and conflict and suffering and death, he yearns for another condition in which he would not have to face them. When the question is posed, "Where do you come from?", though, he cannot say that he once existed in that other condition, and when the question is posed, "Where are you going?", he cannot say that he is going to return to it once again. All he can say is that he yearns for it as though it were his true home.

If he speaks of ecstasy rather than selfhood, however, if he speaks of the joy he finds on the spiritual adventure, then he can say that it comes from God and it carries him toward God. The ecstasy is like a new selfhood, a second selfhood. To enter upon the spiritual adventure is, in the language of the Gospel of John, to be "born anew," to be "born of the Spirit."[30] When Jesus says, "The wind blows where it wills, and you hear the sound of it, but you do not know whence it comes or whither it goes," he goes on to say, "so it is with everyone who is born of the Spirit." In becoming caught up in the spiritual adventure, one does gain the "whence" and "whither" for which one yearned, and yet one does not escape the human condition as one yearned, but has to pass through circumstance and guilt and conflict and suffering and death in order to go from the "whence" to the "whither." The nostalgia and the joy thus are not related as wish and fulfillment but more as wistfulness and passion.

"The passion of man is the reverse of that of Christ," Sartre has said, "for man loses himself as man that God may be born."[31] The passion of man thus described, though, is what we have been calling the "loneliness of the human condition," the "nostalgia." Man loses himself as man in that he yearns for another condition in which he would not have to face circumstance and guilt and conflict and suffering and death. It is more wistfulness than passion. Only when he enters upon the spiritual adventure does it become real passion, but then it is no longer "the reverse of that of Christ." It is, rather, the same as the passion of Christ. It is a losing of himself as God that man may be born. It is a going through the circumstance and

guilt and conflict and suffering and death of the human condition. It is a going from God to God by way of the human
condition, a becoming flesh, as in the saying, "And the Word
became flesh and dwelt among us."

The word "passion" here is being used in its double meaning
of desire and suffering. There is, first, an ineffectual desire that
yearns to escape from suffering, a desire that is not really passion but wistfulness. Then there is a powerful desire that is
willing to go through suffering, a desire that is truly passionate.
"Passion," then, is that willingness to go through and it is also
the actual going through. There is joy in the willingness to go
through, the joy that is "to feel in oneself an excess of strength"
and "to know for certain that you are fulfilling the will of
God," and there is joy to which one comes by actually going
through, the joy that is "the cessation of pain"; but there is
pain in going through. What good is it to go through pain,
though, if all one comes to is "the cessation of pain"? If it is
worthwhile going through the situations of a human life, then
one must come to something more than a simple cessation of
pain. One must come to something greater in which the pain
ceases. That something more or something greater, it seems, is
the sense of being loved and being understood.

"God is spirit," therefore, seems to mean that God is found
in the joy of loving and knowing and in the joy of being loved
and being known. One goes from God to God by going from
joy to joy. To go from loving and knowing to being loved and
being known, nevertheless, one must pass through pain, the
pain of aloneness that appears in each of the situations that
make up the human condition. One comes to ecstasy, a joy of
loving and knowing that carries one outside oneself, and yet
one comes to selfhood, for the fullness of joy is in being loved
and being known. Still, the selfhood one comes to is a new
selfhood, a selfhood of joy rather than of loneliness.

There is a kind of joy already in the loneliness itself, the joy that C. S. Lewis defines as "an unsatisfied desire which is itself more desirable than any other satisfaction."[32] It is as much a sadness as a joy, though, and is felt at times as a sharp pang of nostalgia, of wistfulness. It is a sense that things could be otherwise than they are. It points beyond "how things stand" and beyond the thought that "God is how things stand." At the same time it belongs itself to "how things stand." It is the element in our experience that makes it impossible for us to take "how things stand" for granted. It is what makes us uneasy with the human condition and thus aware that there is a human condition. It is the thing that gives circumstance and guilt and conflict and suffering and death their sting. It is "from God and of God and towards God" in the way that nostalgia is "from and of and towards" the home or the past period or the irrecoverable condition for which it yearns.

It changes into the joy of loving and knowing when one enters upon the spiritual adventure, a joy that is ecstatic, that carries one beyond oneself, beyond the human condition. That joy is a condition of being caught up in the adventure, absorbed in the spiritual journey. It is beyond the loneliness of the human condition insofar as it is powerful rather than ineffectual, passionate rather than wistful. Otherwise it is very much the same longing for God. Still, being powerful and passionate, it is no longer a weak desire to escape but a strong desire to go through and emerge. It goes with a sense that "all things are possible" and "God *is* that all things are possible." One is no longer in the state that Sartre is speaking from when he says, "Man is impossible,"[33] the state of ineffectual longing, but has passed into a state of passionate hope where one can say, "Man is possible."

When one actually begins to realize that possibility by going through and emerging from the situations of one's life, then the joy becomes one of being loved and being known, a fullness of joy. One can say, "God is spirit" at each stage, seeing what the relationship with God does at each stage to the "flesh" of the human condition, how at first it is a weak longing to escape, then a passionate hope of going through, then an actual going through and emerging. At each stage "The wind blows where it wills, and you hear the sound of it, but you do not know whence it comes or whither it goes," and God at each stage is the "whence" and the "whither," but the wind changes. At first it is the wind of loneliness, then it is the wind of love, and finally it is the wind of being loved. The experience of being loved and being known, however, carries one into a new world, a world of shadows as well as of light. There is Rilke's warning: "To be loved means to be consumed, to love is to give light with inexhaustible oil. To be loved is to pass away, to love is to endure."[34] We have been examining the knowing of God that comes out of loving. Let us go on now to examine the knowing that comes out of being known and being loved.

3

The Heart's Vision

"THERE is a dream dreaming us,"[1] a Bushman once told
Laurens van der Post. We are part of a dream, according to
this, part of a vision. What is more, we can become aware of it.
Although we are far removed from the Bushmen and their
vision, it seems we can indeed come to a sense of being
dreamed, being seen, being known. Our mind's desire is to
know, to understand; but our heart's desire is intimacy, to be
known, to be understood. To see God with our mind would be
to know God, to understand God; but to see God with our
heart would be to have a sense of being known by God, of
being understood by God.

If there is a dream dreaming us, it will be God's vision of us,
and if we have a sense of being part of that dream, it will be
our heart's vision of God. Nicholas of Cusa in his *Vision of
God*, while speaking of our vision of God, speaks even more of
God's vision of us.[2] He has it that our seeing God consists of
our having a sense of God seeing us: to see God is to see one
who sees; it is to have an experience of being seen. It is like

looking at one of those portraits, he says, where the eyes are so contrived as to follow the beholder wherever he moves. No matter where the beholder stands, the eyes of the portrait seem to be looking at him. Or better, we could say, it is like feeling the gaze of another person, feeling the gaze without seeing the other's eyes. Or it can be like meeting the gaze of another. Or it can even be like looking into the eyes of another and seeing there the pupil, the *pupilla*, the "little doll," the tiny image of oneself reflected in the other's eyes.

Until now our solitary man's experience of the spiritual adventure has been essentially an experience of loving and knowing. The kindling of his heart has been an experience of loving, of longing for intimacy with God; the illumining of his mind has been an experience of knowing, of seeing with his mind the "from and of and towards" of the love. Now, if he lets his experience become an illumining of the heart, a vision of the heart, he will be letting it become an experience of being known and being loved. Before he gave his heart over to the longing for intimacy with God, such an experience could have been unwelcome, perhaps even hateful and terrifying. Nietzsche, in *Thus Spake Zarathustra*, has Zarathustra encounter the "ugliest man," the man who killed God:

"I recognize you well," he said in a voice of bronze, "you are the murderer of God! Let me go. You could not bear him who saw you—who always saw you through and through, you ugliest man! You took revenge on this witness!"[3]

Let us envision our solitary man going over his experience with this in mind, both his earlier experience of loneliness and languishing before he entered upon the spiritual adventure and his later experience of the love and passion of the adventure itself. Let us see what he will see with his heart.

I. A LONE MAN'S VISION OF A LONE GOD

Before our solitary man entered upon the spiritual adventure, God seemed inaccessible to him, but he himself felt inaccessible to others. He was in a situation like that implied in the phrase "as inaccessible as God or thou." God was as inaccessible as he, and he was as inaccessible as God. He was like K. in Kafka's novel *The Castle*. God will have appeared to him much as the Castle appeared to K.:

> When K. looked at the Castle, often it seemed to him as if he were observing someone who sat quietly there gazing in front of him, not lost in thought and so oblivious of everything, but free and untroubled, as if he were alone with nobody to observe him, and yet must notice that he was observed, and all the same remained with his calm not even slightly disturbed; and really—one did not know whether it was cause or effect—the gaze of the observer could not remain concentrated there, but slid away.[4]

This is a lone man's vision of a lone God. It is a God who sees and who can be seen, but who is nevertheless inaccessible to human beings. It is a God who sees everything, for if everything is the "will of God," as in the common notion, then nothing escapes his notice as he sits "quietly there gazing in front of him." He is "not lost in thought and so oblivious of everything." Moreover, if everything is the "will of God," if things beyond human control are "acts of God," if the afflicted person is a "child of God," as in the common notion, then human beings can observe God at work. They do not see God himself, it is true, but they see what he wills and what he does, and they can pass judgment too, if they dare, on what he wills and does. God, nevertheless, is "free and untroubled," for God cannot be reached by their observations, their judgments, their actions. It is "as if he were alone with nobody to observe him."

For it is impossible to hold God in one's gaze, to force him out of his standpoint into the standpoint of one's own observation and judgment—"the gaze of the observer could not remain concentrated there, but slid away."

This is a solitary man's vision of God. Yet it could also be a description of the solitary man himself. It describes him as he was before he entered upon the spiritual adventure. He saw God as "free and untroubled." Yet he himself was not all longing and loneliness. There was something about him, too, that was free and untroubled. Is it that he knew already with one side of his being the joy he longed for with the other? Does the longing arise out of the joy?

How can a solitary person be free and untroubled? Sometimes one sees what appears to be a happy aloneness in another person and is drawn toward the other in the hope of sharing it. The other seems like a child playing alone, taking delight in all passing things, letting each thing happen, not holding on to anything but letting each pass in its turn. One is reminded of the recurrent line in Genesis: "and God saw that it was good."⁵ It is as though this happy and childlike being sees the coming and going of all things with the eyes God saw the original creation. One could envision God also to be like a child playing, taking delight in all things, letting each one come and go; one hesitates to do so because it would seem to imply a lack of self-consciousness in God. When one approaches the human counterpart of such a God, however, one finds that one cannot really share this happiness simply by being close to the other person, that it is indeed an aloneness, though it is happy. One feels like K. trying to hold the Castle in his gaze. Somehow, in spite of being alone, the other is communing with all things. One feels isolated from things oneself and unable, therefore, to share in the other's vision. One would have to learn to commune with all things, would have to dis cover that happiness for oneself, before one could come back and commune with this happy solitary.

One finds oneself usually, let us say, in the stance of a man before others, concerned primarily about one's relationship with others. In that stance there can be a loneliness, an unhappy aloneness, that goes with being rejected by others or failing to win their acceptance. One lives in hope of acceptance and fear of rejection. One finds relief from the burden of that hope and fear in another stance, let us say, that of a man before himself, especially when one is alone and recollects the events of one's day or maybe retraces the course of one's whole life. It is another place to stand. The hope of acceptance and the fear of rejection become remote there, for one is concerned primarily about one's relationship with oneself. There can be a loneliness there too, nevertheless, that goes with self-rejection or a lack of wholehearted self-acceptance. If one could only accept oneself with a whole heart, one feels, one could get beyond oneself. Both of these standpoints, that before others and that before oneself, are stances of self-consciousness. It is the self that is before others or before oneself. If one could only step into oneself and be oneself, then the self would disappear from in front of one and the world would open up; one would pass from the introspective life into the contemplative life.

Contemplation, one sees from this vantage point just short of it, is the stance of happy aloneness. It is a standpoint where one is neither before others nor before oneself but where everything is before one, where one is like someone "gazing in front of him, not lost in thought and so oblivious of everything, but free and untroubled, as if he were alone with nobody to observe him." It is not a lack of self-consciousness, as one had originally feared. Rather, one has to pass through and beyond the standpoints of self-consciousness to reach it. One has to go from a consciousness of oneself to a willingness to be oneself. When that willingness is there, one steps into oneself, into the mirror image of oneself that has been blocking one's view, and one becomes able to see the universe, to commune with all things.

On further reflection one realizes that there have already been moments in one's life when one has seen things with such a vision, when one has taken delight in passing things and has been oneself a child playing. There is, in fact, a side of one's being that always sees things this way, like the side of the moon that is always facing the earth, and another side that almost never sees things this way, like the other side of the moon that is always facing away from the earth. The side that takes delight in all things is the unselfconscious side of one's being. The other side, the self-conscious side, can come to such a vision, it seems, only by an act of willingness, a wholehearted *Yes* to oneself. The turning of the self-conscious side to contemplation is like the libration of the moon, the oscillating motion that brings the far side of the moon around, first one way and then the other, so that a bit of either edge faces the earth. Thus the self-conscious side of one's being gets only a glimpse of contemplation by turning to it again and again. That glimpse, nevertheless, may be the best indication one has of what God is like. One's unselfconscious side is truly a child playing and seems to be lacking in consecutive thought and moral purpose. The glimpse that one's self-conscious side obtains, on the contrary, is won through a consciousness and a willingness.

Still, what one contemplates now is not God but the world. One does not see God, but at most sees what God sees. It is perhaps a sharing in God's own vision of the world. It is not a cold contemplation, as the image of the moon facing the earth might suggest, but a warm contemplation, a communing with things. There is a wisdom of the earth that one learns from communing. It is not all joy, as one first imagined, seeing the happy person who took delight in all passing things, letting them come and go. Instead there is a mixture of joy and sorrow, the joy of the coming and the sorrow of the going, the joy of life and the sorrow of death. One wonders then whether God too knows sorrow. The great discourses on God, from Aquinas to Spinoza, have usually ended on the theme of God's blessedness, envisioning it to be pure joy. Sharing what may well be God's own vision of the world, however, one sees both joy and sorrow; and one doesn't just observe it, one communes with all beings and actually shares in the joy and the sorrow.

If one were simply to turn toward God, to turn with the self-conscious side of one's being that faces away from the earth like the far side of the moon, one might feel that one was turning toward an inaccessible observer of the earth like Kafka's Castle. One would be turning out of the loneliness of the man before others and the man before himself and into the loneliness of the man before God. If, on the other hand, one were to turn that side of one's being, like the librating moon, first toward the earth and then toward God, one might well feel one was turning rather toward someone who shares in all the joys and sorrows of the earth. It is the self-conscious side of one's being that longs for God, the side that experiences the loneliness. Yet the longing seems to arise out of the communion with all beings that the unselfconscious side experiences. The longing is a longing for communion, and one knows already in one's unselfconscious being what communion is like. If the self-conscious side librates toward the earth, the communing becomes a self-conscious experience, and the longing itself, the librating back toward God, is affected; the vision that goes with it is changed.

One's vision before one goes through this librating motion is an inaccessible gaze. One is like Amalia, the one character in

Kafka's story who has the courage utterly to reject the Castle. Her gaze "was never leveled exactly on the object she was looking at, but in some disturbing way always a little past it."[6] The inaccessible gaze, it seems, will not meet the gaze of another. The inaccessible God sees and is seen but will not meet one's gaze. Or he is one whose gaze one will not meet. When a person says *No* to the longing for communion with God, like Nietzsche's "ugliest man," then he is unwilling to meet the gaze of God. When he says neither *Yes* nor *No*, like our solitary man before he gave his heart over to the longing for communion, then apparently it is God who will not meet the gaze of man. When a person says *Yes*, like our solitary man when he enters upon the spiritual adventure, then both God and man seem willing.

When one goes through the librating motion then, turning to the earth and back to God, one actually does seem to meet the gaze of God. To say neither *Yes* nor *No* to the longing for communion with God is to remain in the first moment, when one has turned toward God and has found God inaccessible. To say *No* is to remain in the second moment, when one has turned away from God to the earth. To say *Yes* is to come to the third moment, when one has turned back again to God and has found God accessible. For, having looked in the direction God is looking, toward the earth, one seems to know what God is seeing when one looks back again, as though one were looking into his eyes and seeing the earth and oneself reflected there.

To meet the gaze of God, short of death, is to have an experience not so much of knowing, it seems, as of being known. "Now we see through a glass darkly," the Apostle Paul says, "but then face to face: now I know in part, but then shall I know even as also I am known."[7] Jorge Luis Borges calls these "the tremulous words of a man who knows himself to be naked to his entrails under God's watchfulness."[8] It is this experience of being known by God, of being naked to one's entrails under God's watchfulness, that is the heart's vision of God. I do not fully meet the gaze of God until death, when "I shall know even as also I am known." Meanwhile I meet it during life when "I know in part," when I know that I am known.

2. "GOD IS NOT SOLITARY"

"God is not solitary,"[9] Aquinas says. If I am known, then I am accessible to God. And if I know that I am known, then God is accessible to me. Aquinas said God was not solitary, it is true, thinking of the Christian doctrine of the Trinity, that there are three persons in the one God: Father and Son and Holy Spirit. What we have in the experience of being known and understood is not the doctrine of the Trinity but, perhaps we could say, the roots of that doctrine. It is the human experience of intimacy with God, of being accessible to God in the loneliest depths of one's being and of having access thereby to God. It points to the intimacy that is seen within God in that doctrine: "No one knows the Son except the Father, and no one knows the Father except the Son."[10] It describes a man who stands in the place of the Son.

Until now we have been calling the man we have been envisioning a "solitary man." Now we are seeing, or he is seeing, that he is not solitary after all. He is not solitary and his God is not solitary. For he is known by his God, and through his sense of being known he knows his God. Before he had this sense of being known he did indeed feel solitary. He had only the sense of a loneliness that could not be reached by intimacy with other human beings, a loneliness that he took to be a longing for communion with God. Then when he gave his heart over to the longing, the loneliness became love. So also when he gave his mind over to the desire to know God, the yearning of the mind became love. His mind's desire was to know; his heart's desire was to be known. Now when he begins to have a sense of being known and of knowing by being known, the love is becoming friendship. It is no longer simply a longing for communion; it is communion. It is no longer simply a longing for intimacy; it is intimacy. It is a loving and being loved, a knowing and being known, a to-and-fro.

When God laughs to the soul and the soul laughs back to God, Meister Eckhart says, the Trinity is born:

Indeed I say, the soul will bring forth Person if God laughs to her and she laughs back to him. To speak in parable, the Father laughs to the Son and the Son laughs back to the Father; and this laughter begets liking, and liking begets joy, and joy begets love, and love begets Person, and Person begets the Holy Spirit.[11]

This is a vision of the heart. It is the heart seeing and experiencing the friendship, the communion, the intimacy, the to-and-fro between God and the human being. The soul stands in the place of the Son. Eckhart is thinking here of Jesus as the Son and of the soul standing in his place in relationship to the Father. The laughter that comes from God to the soul and goes from the soul to God seems to be the same as "the love" that is "from God and of God and towards God." For Eckhart the laughter is liking, is joy, is love, is Person, is the Holy Spirit.

Without the doctrine of the Trinity, there are simply these three in the experience: God, the human being, and the love. The sense of God laughing to the soul goes with the sense of being known by God. When the gods laugh in Homer, it is because they are immortal and human beings are only mortal. It is "Homeric laughter," inextinguishable, irrepressible laughter. When God laughs in the Scriptures (in the Psalms), he laughs at the enemies of the just man. It is derisive, mocking laughter. Here in the experience of God laughing to the soul and the soul laughing back to God, God laughs with a human being rather than at him. It is a shared laughter. Instead of being known without knowing, instead of being merely the butt of laughter, the human being knows by being known, is knowingly rather than unknowingly known. So he shares in the laughter. Moreover, in being known he has the sense of being understood with compassionate understanding. So to him the laughter is the compassionate and sympathetic laughter of humor rather than the derisive and mocking laughter of wit. It is the laughter of "liking" and "joy" and "love." To be known by God and to be loved by God are, in his experience, one and the same.

If we put the experience in terms of the Trinity, as Eckhart does, something further comes to light, namely that the love is not only "from God" and "towards God" but also "of God." It is God's own love. If God laughs to the soul, the love is "from God." If the soul laughs back to God, the love is "towards God." But if the laughter is not only "love" but "Person" and "the Holy Spirit," the love is "of God," is God's own love. We have come across the idea already, and without any thought of a Trinity, both in the old man's words to Lawrence and in Spinoza's words, "The intellectual love of the mind towards God is that very love of God whereby God loves Himself." I have passed over the idea so far without comment because there is a grave difficulty in it. How can the love be God's love when it arises out of one's consent to one's own loneliness for God, when it is a transformation of the basic loneliness of the human condition?

One solution is to separate the love from the loneliness, to deny that the one is a transformation of the other, to call the love "Agape," the name for love in the New Testament, and to call the loneliness "Eros," the name for love in the dialogues of Plato.[12] It seems, nevertheless, that the love is a transformation of the loneliness, that Agape is a transformation of Eros, for when one does give one's heart over to the loneliness for God, as the man we have been envisioning has done, one does actually experience a transformation of loneliness into love. On the other hand, when one comes to a sense of being known by God, as we are envisioning now, one comes also to a sense of being loved by God, and it appears that the kindling of one's heart, the love, has become an illumining of one's heart, a sense of being known and being loved. And when one has the sense of being loved, it appears that one is experiencing a love that is "of God," that one is experiencing God's own love. One could conclude that one's heart is kindled and illumined by God's own love, or one could conclude, more cautiously, that the kindling and the illumining of the heart is a human experience of God's love.

Another and opposite solution is to say that the loneliness itself is "of God," that it is God's own loneliness, that the loneliness is an experience of what the Baal Shem Tov calls the "exile of God's glory,"[13] that God's glory (the Shekinah) has been exiled from God in the creation of the world and that it (or she) seeks always to return and be reunited with God. When, like the man we have been envisioning, a human being consents to the loneliness and the longing for God, then, according to this, "he unites the bridegroom with the bride—the Holy God with the Indwelling Glory."[14] In such a vision the thing that is "from and of and towards" God is the Shekinah, the glory of God, and there are "holy sparks"[15] of that glory in all human beings and in all things in the world. Here, too, it seems we could say that the loneliness is not so much the glory itself as a human experience of the glory in exile.

If the love is not God's love itself but a human experience of it, if the loneliness is not God's glory itself in exile but a human experience of it, then we are talking not about God but about the human experience of God. When God laughs to the soul and the soul laughs back to God, it is not the Trinity that is born but the human experience of the Trinity. It is not the Holy Spirit that is born but the human experience of the Holy Spirit. The laughter or the love coming "from God" is the human experience of the Father, going "towards God" is the human experience of the Son, and being "of God" is the human experience of the Holy Spirit. The Trinity, we might surmise from this, is seen by the heart; the doctrine of the Trinity arises out of a vision of the heart. It is the vision of a man who stands in the place of the Son and calls God "Father," or better, who calls God "Abba," the intimate name for "Father," as Jesus did, who experiences within himself "the Spirit of adoption, whereby we cry, Abba, Father," "the Spirit of his Son, crying, Abba, Father."[16]

To stand in the place of the Son and to know what it is to stand in that place is to see the Son with the vision of the heart. It is, in the language of John's Gospel, to "behold the glory" of the Son. The glory is linked in the Gospel with the figure of Jesus and is understood to be the glory of being the Son of God. "We have beheld his glory," John says, "glory as of the only Son from the Father."[17] It is like the Shekinah: it was with God before the world began, is in the world, and returns to God. "And now, Father," Jesus prays at the end of his life on earth, "glorify thou me in thy own presence with the glory which I had with thee before the world was made."[18] When Jesus says "I am" in John's Gospel, he seems to be speaking of that glory, but it is a glory that he can share with others, letting them stand in his place in relationship with God: "The glory which thou hast given me I have given to them," giving them "power to become children of God."[19]

If we link the glory with the loneliness of the human condition, then the figure of Jesus appears to be the embodiment of a universal experience, a sense of coming from God and being of God and longing to return to God. If we link it with the love, then Jesus appears to be the embodiment of an experience common to the friends of God, a sense of to-and-fro, of intercourse, of childlike intimacy with God. If we link it with Jesus himself, as the Gospel of John does, then Jesus appears not just to be illumined by the loneliness and the love but to illumine them. He seems to increase their contrast, to brighten the love, to deepen the shadows of the loneliness, "And the light shines in the darkness, and the darkness did not comprehend it."[20]

Say the man we have been envisioning does link the glory with Jesus himself. Say he does come to "behold the glory" in the figure of Jesus. As he does so, the light becomes brighter for him, and the darkness becomes darker. Now he is coming to share fully in the vision of John's Gospel. The loneliness, that by itself might be taken simply as a sign of one's origin and destiny, of being created by God and for God, becomes something darker, a sign of one's exile from God. He begins to see the link between the loneliness and the dark forces at work in the human being: the languishing, the pining, the ineffectual longing that is the loneliness appears to undercut and subvert everything in the human being, like a pervasive dissatisfaction, to turn love into indifference, desire into disgust, joy into sadness, daring into fear, hope into despair. It appears to be the source of the seemingly causeless frustration, anger, resentment, and violence that can well up in a human being. On the other hand, the love, that by itself might seem simply the realization of one's capacity for God, becomes in its contrast with the loneliness a return to God from one's exile. It promises to heal the languishing, to transform the dark forces, to bring one from indifference and disgust and sadness and fear and despair to love and desire and joy and daring and hope. It seems able to go to the root of the frustration and violence and make one heart-free and heart-whole. In the contrast, the love becomes so bright that it becomes laughter; the loneliness becomes so dark that it becomes misery.

"One may well know God without knowing one's misery, and one may know one's misery without knowing God," Pascal says, "but one cannot know Jesus Christ without knowing at once God and one's misery."[21] Nietzsche's "ugliest man" knew his misery without knowing God, or without wanting to be known by God. The man we have been envisioning was until now one who knew God without fully realizing his own misery, but he was willing to be known by God, and now he has come to the point of knowing his misery and knowing Jesus Christ. It is his willingness to be known by God that has made the difference. When one is willing to be known by God, one is willing to be known in one's darkest depths, and one is willing to know those depths oneself.

There are three parts to the heart's vision we have come to, and all three of them seem to arise out of a sense of being known and a willingness to be known by God. One is that of knowing God, knowing from being known, knowing God to have access to human beings and by that very access to be accessible in turn to them. Another is that of knowing one's misery, knowing it from the sense of being known in it by God, from being knowingly and willingly accessible to God in one's darkest reaches. And the third is that of knowing Jesus, finding God accessible in him and oneself accessible to God in him, when one stands in his relationship to God. Pascal seems right to say "one cannot know Jesus Christ without knowing at once God and one's misery," for one cannot find God accessible in him without thereby knowing God and one cannot find oneself accessible to God in him without thereby knowing one's misery. It is one thing, nevertheless, to know one's darkness willingly, like the man we are envisioning, and another to know it unwillingly, like the "ugliest man." It is the other two parts of the vision, it seems, knowing God and knowing Jesus, that make it possible for one to be willing or to remain willing when one comes to see one's darkness.

That darkness is not immediately and entirely dissipated, one can see, when one passes from the loneliness to the love, even though that passing is truly a passing from darkness to light. Instead, the love is a kindling of one's mind and heart that gives one the willingness to know and the courage to face one's darkness. It is an illumining of mind and heart that enables one to enter one's darkness and find one's way in it. Let us suppose the man we have been envisioning does set out now to face and to know his darkness, to enter it and find his way in it, with the warmth and the light of the love. He is no longer a solitary man. He feels that he is accessible to God and that he has access to God. In entering his own darkness he is in effect becoming accessible to human beings and gaining access to them, for the darkness has been the barrier between him and others.

4

God in the Darkness

"IN Bimini, on the old Spanish Main," Loren Eiseley tells, "a black girl once said to me, 'Those as hunts treasure must go alone, at night, and when they find it they have to leave a little of their blood behind them.' "[1] That is the way also with entering one's inner darkness. One must go alone, in the dark, and when one finds what one is seeking one has to leave a little of one's blood behind.

What may one hope to find? "Man cannot live without an enduring trust in something indestructible in himself," Kafka says. "Yet while doing that he may all his life be unaware of that indestructible thing and of his trust in it."[2] If one enters one's inner darkness, it seems, one may hope to penetrate the unawareness and find that indestructible something within oneself and also one's continual reliance on it. One may hope, Jung says, "to find out what it is that supports him when he can no longer support himself." The "highest and most decisive experience," according to Jung, is "to be alone." "Only this experience can give him an indestructible foundation."[3] When he does find an indestructible foundation, however, he finds that he is not alone after all. "The indestructible is one: it is every human being individually and at the same time all human beings collectively," Kafka says; "hence the marvelous indissoluble alliance of mankind."⁴ One goes alone, but one may hope to be unalone; one goes in the dark, but one may hope that one's indestructible foundation will come to light; one has to leave a little of one's blood behind one, but one may hope to find support where one can no longer support oneself.

There are two things for us to do if all this about the indestructible in man is true. One is to find out how the indestructible foundation and a person's reliance on it is concealed from him. The other is to find out how it is common and may be shared. The first is a matter of coming to self-knowledge or, perhaps more accurately, of coming to a knowledge of the soul. The second is a matter of coming by way of the soul to others.

1. "ONLY GOD ENTERS INTO THE SOUL"

"One who knows himself is stronger in knowing than one who knows his Lord," Al-Alawi says, "and one who is veiled from himself is more heavily veiled than one who is veiled from his Lord."⁵ To know the love the old man spoke of to Lawrence, it seems, is to know one's Lord; to know the loneliness that is its root in the human being, on the other hand, is to know oneself. The man we have been envisioning has come to know the truth of the old man's words, "The love is from God and of God and towards God," and he has been gradually led toward saying also, "The loneliness is from God and of God and towards God"; but if that is true of the loneliness he has not yet fully realized it. His movement in the spiritual adventure has been to go from the loneliness to the love and only afterward in the light of the love to go back into the roots of loneliness. The longing that is the essence of the loneliness lasts on in the love. Even now that he has found an intimacy with God, let us say, he still feels in himself a longing for intimacy. "What do I want?" he asks himself. He still does not know his heart.

He is not "veiled from his Lord," for he has come to a sense of being known and loved by God. Yet he is "veiled from himself," for the sense of being known and loved has not yet fulfilled his longing for intimacy. What he must do, it appears, is use the sense of being known to know his own heart. "The eye with which I see God is the same eye with which God sees me," Meister Eckhart says. "My eye and God's eye are one eye and one vision or seeing and one knowing and one loving."[6] I can see God with the same eye God sees me even before death, it seems, by using the sense of being known by God to know God; but I can also use that eye to see myself, to see in the dark of the human heart.

If I enter the darkness of my own heart, however, I am entering the region of my being where I am ordinarily inaccessible to human beings; I am entering where God enters. I am using the sense of being accessible to God to become accessible to myself and to others. "Only God enters into the soul," Aquinas says.[7] Here is where we encounter the two dangers we spoke of earlier, that of erasing the line between God and self, and that of erasing the line between self and others. Let us imagine our no longer solitary man entering his soul. Let us imagine him using his sense of being known and being loved to know and love. Let us see how he could meet the dangers, what he might do with lines between God and self and others.

"Only God enters into the soul." If that is true, it may be a clue as to why the soul is dark. There is a deep loneliness, we have been saying, that is not taken away even when one is very intimate with another human being, and that loneliness is a longing for intimacy, for communion. It is, we have been thinking, a longing for communion with God. Yet the longing itself does not know this, does not know that it longs for God. It does not differentiate between communion with God and communion with other human beings. It is an undifferentiated longing for intimacy. And thus it is dark; it is pervaded with unknowing. It will look to other human beings for an intimacy that can only be had with God. It will expect others to enter into the soul, to understand one in full (*im ganzen* as Kafka said), to enter where only God can enter, to understand as only God can understand, to love as only God can love. When they fail to do so, the longing will be disappointed and will tend to turn against them for failing it, and it will tend to turn against the self for causing the failure and the apparent rejection by others. What began by being an unknowing, a darkness, ends by becoming also an unloving, a coldness toward others and toward the self. In the unknowing, though, it appears that it is others who are unloving, for they appear to refuse the intimacy, the communion that is sought. At the same time, it appears that the self is incapable of love, incapable of entering into any deep communion with others, or perhaps so unlovely, so unloveable, that others will not enter into communion with it.

Say the man we have been envisioning finds all these feelings within himself. There is the darkness: he finds himself looking to other human beings to take away the deep loneliness that only God can reach. And there is the coldness: he finds a bitterness against others, especially those with whom he had most desired to be intimate, a bitter coldness, and a sense of being circled himself by a ring of cold. He is no longer solitary, we have said, but part of him does not know, he discovers now, and does not love, at least with discerning love, what the other part of him knows and loves.

His realizing all this is already a knowing. It is a knowing of the unknowing, a knowledge of ignorance. One thinks of Socrates whose wisdom consisted of knowing that he did not know, of knowing that "Only God is wise."[8] In fact, we can see a parallel between the two sayings, "Only God is wise" and "Only God enters into the soul." A human being becomes wise and enters into his own soul, it seems, only to the extent that he becomes aware of his own unknowing. His awareness does not take away the unknowing, does not turn the night into day. Rather, it is like seeing in the dark. The man we are envisioning finds unknowing in the form of undifferentiated longing. Even after he has become aware of it, though, and has seen how it goes to human beings for an intimacy that can only be had with God, and has seen also how the disappointment it meets leads to bitterness, he finds himself still expecting other human beings to make him unalone and still being hurt when they fail to do so. There is still the bitterness, still the blind seeking. He has come up against something in himself that will not yield to knowing.

It may yet yield to loving. Undifferentiated longing is already a kind of love, an undiscerning love. Forgiving, on the other hand, releasing others from the demand placed upon them by undiscerning love, is love that is discerning. "Who can forgive sins but God only?"[9]—the question that arises in the hearts of the scribes when Jesus tells the paralytic his sins are forgiven—seems to contain a thought paralleling that of the two sayings, "Only God is wise" and "Only God enters into the soul." Jesus has it, however, that human beings can forgive, as when he teaches his disciples to pray "Forgive us our debts, as we forgive our debtors" or "Forgive us our sins, for we also forgive everyone that is indebted to us."[10] Say the man we are envisioning releases or tries to release others from the demand to make him unalone, forgives or tries to forgive them the debt that undiscerning love has placed upon them. Say he experiences being forgiven himself as he forgives, being released as he releases, being freed from the bitterness toward others and toward himself in which he has been held. Say he does this again and again, releasing and being released, then holding and being held, then again releasing and being released, as he goes back and forth between discerning and undiscerning love.

In the moments of discerning love it seems he does indeed know what God knows and love what God loves. Actually he doesn't know more than he knew before, he just knows it with more of him, with a part of him that was blind to it before. He knew already with his mind that the longing was for God. Now he knows it with the longing itself. The longing knows in moments when it recognizes its own fulfillment, but then in other moments it relapses into unknowing. In moments of undiscerning love he would have to express the longing in something like the African love song we mentioned:

I walk alone.

There is in the song, at least as he would sing it, a cry to others, an appeal to make one unalone. And when they fail to do so, the cry becomes a grudge, a complaint against others and against oneself. In moments of discerning love, on the other hand, when he is able to cease holding the grudge, to release others and be released himself, he might dare to sing instead:

I walk with God,

echoing the sentences in Genesis, "Enoch walked with God" and "Noah walked with God,"[11] where the cry would be one of fulfillment.

Releasing and being released is like dying, like willingly dying. It is like going through the letting go of everyone and everything that one is called upon to go through on one's deathbed. There is great aloneness then too: I am dying while others, even those closest to me, go on living. There can be great darkness and coldness also, expecting others to take away that final aloneness, feeling bitter and abandoned when they inevitably fail. Going through all this in the midst of life, like the man we are envisioning, means going through death before one dies, going through at least the letting-go that death imposes. Walking with God, then, means walking through death. It means living with death behind one rather than ahead of one. The sentence that begins "Enoch walked with God" ends "and he was not, for God took him."

By going through death before one dies, one comes upon something indestructible within oneself. One releases and is released, one goes through death, and yet one still lives. So there is something in one that survives even the letting-go that is called for in death. This is Kafka's "something indestructible" and Jung's "indestructible foundation." Tolstoy, in *The Death of Ivan Ilych*, tells the story of a man who goes through something very similar to what we are envisioning, a living that is pervaded by an unknowing and an unloving, then a dying that is a releasing and a being released. Ivan Ilych goes through the letting-go on his deathbed, it is true, rather than during life. But he comes through into a new life before he actually dies. He sees himself being forced down into a dark sack by death, but when he does let go and does go down into the sack he meets with a surprise. "Where is death?" he asks. He cannot find it anywhere, for he has already gone through it, already gone through at least the letting-go of everyone and everything that it involves. "In place of death there was light."[12] The light is the new life into which he has entered. He takes his last breath a few minutes later, but those last minutes have been a new life of knowing and loving.

When he lets go of everyone and everything and goes down into the dark sack of death, he lets go of every support in his life except the indestructible foundation of his life. He relies on the indestructible foundation alone. So at that point the indestructible foundation and his reliance on it come to light. It becomes clear that he has been relying on it all along, that his reliance on it, as Kafka says, is "enduring." Also it becomes clear that both the indestructible foundation and his reliance on it have been concealed from him by his reliance on everyone and everything else. Nothing is added at this point. Instead, everyone and everything else is subtracted. When he finds that "in place of death" there is "light," however, a new life opens up before him in which the indestructible foundation and his reliance on it are no longer concealed from him. He lives consciously and willingly out of that indestructible foundation from now on, even if he has only a few minutes to live. He still has a relationship to everyone and everything else, but it is changed.

What is the indestructible foundation that comes to light? And what is the new relationship to everyone and everything else? To Kafka the indestructible foundation is the individual himself, and at the same time it is something the individual has in common with everyone and everything else. "It is every human being individually," he says, "and at the same time all human beings collectively." It is not God, according to Kafka. One of the ways in which a person can remain unaware of it, Kafka says, is "to have faith in a personal God."[13] If a person's experience is like that of Ivan Ilych, however, things are the other way around. God is the indestructible foundation, and what conceals God is the individual and what he has in common with everyone and everything else. For his experience is one of dying, of having to let go of everyone and everything, even of his own life. To someone like the man we have been imagining, who is not actually on his deathbed, this will not be as quick and direct as it was for Ivan Ilych. He will have to work his way through everyone and everything, and even through his own life, to find his indestructible foundation. He will have to work his way through life in the human circle, and that may be a long journey. God will not be his whole life until he has found God not only in solitude but also in the human circle.

2. THE HUMAN CIRCLE

Once when heaven and earth were closer, it is said in the traditions of many peoples, there were human beings who walked and spoke with God. Since then heaven and earth have drawn apart from each other, and God and man seldom meet. When they do meet, when a human being does come to walk and speak with God, it is like a new beginning, like starting the human race all over again, like living at the dawn of the world. A further separation has occurred now, we could add, continuing the story. Not only has mankind become separated from God but the individual has become separated from mankind. So now we are at a second remove. An individual may now find himself in a predicament like that of K. in Kafka's novel *The Castle*, always striving to be received into the Castle and never succeeding, then striving at least to be received into the village beneath the Castle and still not succeeding. He may feel that he is sundered both from God and from mankind.

Yet it may be that in stepping outside the human circle and

entering into his own solitude, the individual has come into a region where God is to be found. It may be that he is actually closer to God rather than farther away. He is close to God if, like the man we are envisioning, he sees in his aloneness the possibility of the spiritual adventure. Then his task is to find God in solitude and, after that, come back and find God in the human circle. Instead of taking the human circle as it stands, he has to widen it to include what has been left outside. He has to work his way through the human circle as it stands, to pass through death in the midst of life, to release and be released, in order to live in the larger circle that it can become. The story from this point of view can be told in a different way, as an emergence more than a separation. First there is the emergence of mankind; then there is the emergence of the individual.

The lines between God and self and others, as they are ordinarily seen, appear to have been established by the first emergence, that of mankind from God, when the human circle was created. The line between God and mankind is indeed that of the human circle. God in the common notion is outside the realm of human intercourse, but the only human being who is outside is the "child of God," the afflicted person who has never emerged fully as a human being and never been able to enter fully into the human circle. The line between self and others is the same circle, and it appears whenever one crosses it and enters into the deep solitude where one is not accessible to others. When one comes back again from solitude, however, things can change, the human circle can expand to include what one has found in solitude.

When one comes back from solitude, one may come to discount all lines except those drawn by what we are now calling "discerning love," a longing for God that is knowingly a longing for God, that releases other human beings from fulfilling it, that finds fulfillment in walking with God. There is self-knowledge in knowingly longing for God. If the longing comes to know it longs for God, the individual will become luminous in his aloneness. He will become accessible where he has been dark and inaccessible. To another person he will appear to be living clear down in his heart where before he appeared to be divided against himself. He will seem to be heart-free and heart-whole where before it seemed there was no knowing his heart.

It is ironic that he should become accessible to others only when he releases them from fulfilling his longing for communion. There is knowledge of others, though, in releasing them, just as there is self-knowledge in knowing the longing is for God. He can know in releasing others that all human beings dwell in the same solitude. He already knows that loneliness is the human condition, but he can come to have a compassionate sense of the longing in others. He can know from experience the states in which the longing may exist, what it is like when it is ineffectual, when it becomes powerful, when it is undiscriminating, when it becomes discerning. He can be close to others in a way he never was through ordinary human intercourse. He can be close to them in their aloneness, in their darkness and coldness, in their illumining and their kindling. He will no longer expect them to take away his solitude, knowing they dwell in the same solitude themselves, but neither will it be necessary any more to take it away, for human beings can be near one another even in deep solitude.

Only the One who is not solitary can make one unalone, according to discerning love. There is knowledge of God in that, in finding fulfillment in walking with God. One can understand in that way the last words of Al-Hallaj: "The ecstatic wants only to be alone with his Only One."[14] It is true, the God of Al-Hallaj is a solitary God whereas the God of the man we are envisioning is not solitary. Still, oneness

with God as Al-Hallaj understood it was a "unity of witness,"[15] similar it seems to what we have been calling "knowing what God knows and loving what God loves." The only
real difference is that our no longer solitary man sees himself
entering into an intimacy that already exists within God, the
oneness of the Father and the Son. In being known and loved
he sees himself entering into the intimacy of "no one knows the
Son except the Father," and in knowing and loving he sees
himself entering into that of "no one knows the Father except
the Son."

There is a oneness that is seen before and a oneness that is
seen only after the heart's vision in which "God is not solitary." Before the heart's vision God is the one source from
which all come and to which all return, the One of the mind's
vision, the One to which Spinoza argues, for example, in his
letters to Huyghens on the unity of God.[16] After the heart's
vision, God is the One who is not solitary, and there is the
oneness of which Jesus speaks in the Gospel of John when he
says "I and my Father are one."[17] It is a oneness that makes
one unalone when one enters into it, as when he says "I am not
alone, for the Father is with me."[18] It is a clue to what human
intercourse can become after the individual has emerged from
mankind, as when he prays "that they may be one, even as we
are one: I in them, and thou in me."[19]

Human intercourse, before the emergence of the individual,
has to do with love and work and communal life. It has been
said, in fact, that love and work and communal life are the
fundamental "tasks of life."[20] Each one of them is in reality a
form of interchange between human beings. The individual
emerges in a life, or in history itself, whenever the deep aloneness that we have been speaking of, the aloneness that is not
ordinarily touched in love and work and communal life, becomes so intense that it begins to undermine ordinary human

intercourse and make it seem unsatisfactory, when it seems no longer possible to find fulfillment in love and work and communal life. When that happens, the spiritual adventure that we have been speaking of can begin. Before it happens, God seems outside the human circle, outside the realm of human intercourse, and is understood as in the common notion. After it happens, the human being himself seems outside the human circle. By becoming an individual, entering into the deep aloneness, he seems to have become separated from mankind, unless the human circle itself can be widened somehow to encompass the spiritual adventure.

Inside the human circle as it stands there are the tasks of life, love and work and communal life. Outside it there are the boundary situations that define the human condition, circumstance and conflict and guilt and suffering and death, outside it because these situations drive human beings into deep solitude. When the loneliness that appears in each of these situations becomes love, as we have been envisioning, then it may be possible for the human circle to expand until it includes them. It may be possible for human beings to meet in circumstance and conflict and guilt and suffering and death. "I in them, and thou in me" describes the place where they may meet, the place of the Son, a locus of knowing and being known, of loving and being loved.

What would it be to meet where we are most alone? An image of such a meeting would be that of meeting a "child of God," an afflicted person who lives outside the human circle. Dostoevsky seems to describe such a meeting in *The Idiot*. He set out there to depict a good man, but with the consciousness of the Gospel, "one there is who is good,"[21] and so he imaged the good man as an idiot, a "child of God." Prince Myshkin, the idiot of his story, meets others where they are most alone—in their circumstance, their conflict, their guilt, their suffering, their dying. The whole story takes place in a lucid interval. Myshkin is an epileptic and has just emerged at the beginning of the story from a period of idiocy. At the end he relapses into idiocy once more. In between he is lucid and is able to enter into the human circle. But he brings with him the experience of living outside it in isolation. So he knows how to meet others in their aloneness. Others on their part are drawn to him, drawn by his goodness. He seems to be luminous where they are dark.

Someone once said he never understood the Gospel of John until he read *The Idiot*. The parallel is in the structure of the story. Jesus comes from the world of light into the world of darkness, and then he leaves the world of darkness and returns once more to the world of light. Myshkin comes from the darkness of idiocy into the light of the human circle, and then he leaves the human circle and returns once more to idiocy. At first the one story seems to be the inverse of the other. There is a parallel, nevertheless, as one thinks about it, between the world of light and the darkness of idiocy: in the world of light Jesus is with the Father; in the darkness of idiocy Myshkin is a "child of God." There is also a parallel between Jesus in the world of darkness and Myshkin in the human circle. Jesus is luminous where others are dark, and so some are drawn to the light they see in him while others are repelled by their fear of the light. It is the same with Myshkin: some are drawn to the light in him, others are afraid of it.

Meeting where we are most alone, it is clear from both stories, is at once desirable and fearful. We desire to be understood "in full" (*im ganzen*) and at the same time we fear it. There is a conflict of desire and fear, one could say, as long as the desire for communion is weak and ineffectual. When we enter upon the spiritual adventure, however, there is a choice against fear, and the desire becomes powerful. When we actually do meet where we are most alone, it seems, we meet in the place where Jesus stands in the Gospel of John, the place of the Son, or in the place where Myshkin stands in *The Idiot*, the place of the "child of God" who has entered into the human circle.

There is a deep ambivalence of feeling surrounding the figure of the "child of God." On the one hand, he is afflicted; on the other, he is close to God. There is something at once dreadful and fascinating about him. His affliction is dreadful; his closeness to God is fascinating. So it is as long as he stays outside the human circle. When he enters the human circle, as Dostoevsky's Idiot does, then there is something else. We are forced to make a choice, either to come into the light he casts upon our aloneness or to flee from it. Instead of simply making that choice, *Yes* or *No*, we have imagined a man who himself reenacts the experience of the Idiot, going outside the human circle and then coming inside it again, going into his own darkness and then coming back with the light he has found there. Instead of confronting the Idiot, therefore, we end up standing in his place.

That place is a strange one. If a "child of God" enters the human circle, we can expect him to change everything he finds there: love and work and communal life. But it can appear very difficult, nearly impossible, for him to enter the human circle. Yeats, describing someone on a rather similar threshold, and alluding to Dostoevsky's Idiot, says "he tried out of ambition to change his nature, as though a man should make love who had no heart, but now shock can give him back his heart." To enter the human circle is a shock after living in deep solitude, but only a shock can give him the heart for love and work and communal life. "Only a shock resulting from the greatest possible conflict can make the greatest possible change," Yeats goes on to say. "Nor can anything intervene. He must be aware of nothing but the conflict, his despair is necessary, he is of all men the most tempted—'Eloi, Eloi, why hast thou forsaken me?' "[22] In going outside the human circle he seemed to lose everyone and everything but God. In coming back into the human circle he can seem to lose God, to be forsaken by God.

Let us imagine him entering the human circle. Let us see what shock, what conflict, what despair, what temptation he will encounter. Let us see what he will do with love and work and communal life. He is like Prince Myshkin at the beginning of Dostoevsky's story. He has just emerged from solitude, like Myshkin returning to Russia from his isolation in Switzerland. He is looking forward to entering once again into the human circle, wondering himself what he will encounter, wondering what he will do with love and work and communal life after so much has happened to him in solitude.

5

The Quest of an Unknown Life

ONE who enters the human circle after having lived in deep solitude finds what is to him a mysterious life. It is the same, the other way around, for someone who has lived in the human circle and meets one who has lived in deep solitude. Each may be drawn to the life he sees in the other. The thought that another person possesses a mysterious life that we could share through love, Proust says, is all we need to fall in love:

> To believe a being partakes of an unknown life (*une vie inconnue*) into which love would lead us, this is, of all that must be before love will come to birth, the one thing most needed, and it makes the rest easy.[1]

Indeed we may see "an unknown life" not only in love but also in work and communal life, in each and every form of human intercourse. One who has been living in deep solitude will find an unknown life in the intercourse itself. He will be fascinated by love and work and communal life, will be in love with love, with work, with communal life, and at the same time afraid of each one of them, afraid of the human intercourse that takes place in each of them, fascinated and afraid for the same reason, because they are unfamiliar to him, because human intercourse is strange to him. One who has been living in the human circle, on the other hand, will find an unknown life in solitude or in the solitary. He will be fascinated by the solitude he sees in the solitary, and at the same time afraid of it, desirous and yet fearful of making contact with it by entering into touch with the solitary. The contact he desires and fears will take place through love and work and communal life, but it is not those forms of intercourse themselves that he desires and fears so much as the deep solitude he senses in the other.

Let us imagine a man, therefore, the one we have been envisioning thus far, entering the human circle and coming to terms with the dread and fascination he feels for human intercourse. Let us also imagine a second person, however, who has been living in the human circle and who feels a dread and fascination for solitude. Let us call the life each one knows the life of "self," and let us call the unknown life for each the life of "soul."[2]

I. SELF AND SOUL

When the human circle is the unknown world, as it is for the man we have been envisioning, then self is solitary and soul is not solitary. When solitude is the unknown world, on the other hand, as it is for the second person we are now introducing, then it is soul that is solitary and self that is not solitary. What is self in the one is soul in the other. The first person is alone, like Kafka writing "There is no one here who has an understanding for me in full," and is always seeking to be unalone, "To have even one who had this understanding, for instance a woman, would be to have support from every side. It would be to have God."[3] The second person, on the other hand, is unalone and is always seeking to be alone. "There is no one here who knows how to be alone," we could imagine this second person saying, and "To know how to be alone would be to know how to live without support from every side."

By introducing a second person into our story we are opening up new possibilities, the manifold possibilities of dialogue and interaction, like Aeschylus introducing a second actor into drama where before there had been only one actor and a chorus. If the second person, however, is one who is unalone and seeks to be alone, as we are supposing, while the first person is alone and seeks to be unalone, the dialogue and interaction between them will be like the inner dialogue and intertaction between self and soul within a single person. The first person's self is solitary; the second's is unsolitary. The first person's soul is linked with woman, with support from every side, with God; the second's is linked with independence.

"Who can distinguish darkness from the soul?" Yeats asks in his poem "A Dialogue of Self and Soul."[4] The darkness, it seems, is that of the unknown life, the life of the human circle for the first person, the life of solitude for the second. Let us see how far dialogue between the two persons would bring light into their inner dialogue of self and soul.

Say the second person is a woman, like the woman Camus describes in his story "The Adulterous Woman." Her life has been confined to the human circle. Her "only joy," like that of the woman Camus describes, has been "the knowledge that she was necessary,"[5] necessary to others, needed by them. She has been needed and she has needed that need. She has been living in the one great certainty of human existence, "I am," affirmed ever and again by others and their needs, and has been fleeing from the other great certainty, "I will die." Now, though, she has begun to feel that something is lacking, that her life in the human circle is a kind of confinement, an imprisonment. She longs to go outside the human circle into solitude even though she knows it will mean facing the prospect of her own death. She determines to step outside the human circle, like a married woman stepping outside her marriage. This is her "adultery." In Camus' story it takes the form of intercourse with the night sky:

> Breathing deeply, she forgot the cold, the dead weight of others, the craziness or stuffiness of life, the long anguish of living and dying. After so many years of mad, aimless fleeing from fear, she had come to a stop at last. At the same time, she seemed to recover her roots and the sap again rose in her body, which had ceased trembling. Her whole belly pressed against the parapet as she strained towards the moving sky; she was merely waiting for her fluttering heart to calm down and establish silence within her. The last stars of the constellations dropped their clusters a little lower on the desert horizon and became still. Then, with unbearable gentleness, the water of night began to fill her, drowned the cold, rose gradually from the hidden core of her being and overflowed in wave after wave, rising up even to her mouth full of moans. The next moment, the whole sky stretched out over her, fallen on her back on the cold earth.[6]

Her experience of the human circle, apart from her "only joy," "the knowledge that she was necessary," has been one of "dead weight," of "craziness or stuffiness," of "long anguish." There is "the dead weight of others," the burden of being needed, of having always to be meeting the needs of others, of having always to carry others around on her back, as it were, and never being able to walk free and by herself. There is "the craziness or stuffiness of life," the confinement of her life to the human circle, like being locked up in a room with other people and all the windows closed, finding it more and more difficult to breathe. There is "the long anguish of living and dying," having to live every day with care, having to rise to it every morning and go to bed exhausted from it every night, without any prospect of relief until the day comes when she will be too exhausted to rise to it any more.

When she steps out of the human circle into solitude, on the other hand, it is like walking free, breathing fresh air, becoming carefree. "After so many years of mad, aimless fleeing from fear, she had come to a stop at last." Her great fear while she remained in the human circle was that she would cease to be needed and wanted. She was afraid that if she were not needed it would be as if she did not even exist. When she steps out into solitude, she finds herself outside those needs she thought she needed and yet she finds she does exist after all. "At the same time, she seemed to recover her roots and the sap again rose in her body." For in solitude her existence seems to rise out of her own roots rather than out of the needs of others. "Then, with unbearable gentleness, the water of night began to fill her, rose gradually from the hidden core of her being and overflowed in wave after wave." She is filled in solitude with life, a new life, an unknown life, a life beyond the life she has known in the human circle. Because it is unfamiliar, unknown to her, it is dark; it is "the water of night." Still it is a life that is within her; it rises "from the hidden core of her being."

She is like the woman at the well in the Gospel of John. The "water of night" is like the water Jesus offers to the woman at the well. "Whoever drinks of the water that I shall give him will never thirst," he tells her, "but the water I shall give him will become in him a spring of water welling up to eternal life."[7] The man we have been imagining, however, cannot quite play the role of Jesus in this scene. Jesus begins by saying to the woman, "Give me to drink."[8] The man we are envisioning would have to ask that too, but he would have to pursue that request further than Jesus does, for he too is in search of an unknown life. At first it seems that the life the woman seeks is known to the man and the life the man seeks is known to the woman, but it is not so. She does not seek simply the life of solitude nor he simply that of the human circle, but both seek the total life. And neither of them knows the total life already from experience.

What he knows is not the total life but only that of solitude. He knows what it is to walk alone and what it is to walk with God, but he doesn't know what it is for human beings to meet where they are most alone. The total life is thus more than just solitude plus the human circle. It is the transformation of solitude and of the human circle that takes place when human beings do meet where they are most alone. The woman's image of solitude—intercourse with the night sky—is an image of communion with the unknown. It is true to life, from the man's experience of solitude, except that it leaves out the negative side, the loneliness that one can suffer outside the human circle, the deep loneliness that appears in the boundary situations, death and guilt and suffering and conflict and circumstance. He cannot give her what she seeks, an experience of communion in solitude that is untainted by loneliness. He doubts that such a thing exists unless it exists in that total life he has yet to attain, that meeting of human beings where they are most alone.

His image of human beings meeting where they are most alone, on the other hand, has about the same relation to her experience of the human circle as her image of intercourse with the night sky has to his experience of solitude. It leaves out the negative side of life in the human circle, the burden, the stifling, the weariness of being necessary to others. She cannot give him what he seeks, an experience of deep encounter that is free from the oppression that arises from need and the need to be needed. And she doubts that such a thing exists, just as he doubts her quest, unless it exists in that total life she herself seeks, that communion she envisions with the unknown.

"How is it that you, a Jew, ask a drink of me, a woman of Samaria?"[9] That is the initial response of the woman at the well to Jesus' request, "Give me to drink." But then, when he has described the water he will give her, she says, "Sir, give me this water, that I may not thirst, nor come here to draw."[10] We can imagine something similar happening when someone from solitude begins to speak with someone from the human circle. There is first the problem of comprehending one another, of coming to understand one another's quest. Each is somehow asking the other the equivalent of "Give me to drink." When the one finds with astonishment that the other is seeking a solitude untainted by loneliness, and the other finds with no less astonishment that he is seeking a relationship untainted by need, the question becomes "How is it that you ask this of me?" And the answer is "Because you seem to live the life that I seek." Each one, contemplating the other, asks for the water of the unknown life, "Let me share in the mysterious life you seem to live."

It does not follow from the man's experience that the woman's quest is vain nor from the woman's experience that the man's quest is vain. It is true, there is a negative side to his experience of solitude and to her experience of the human circle, but the loneliness in his experience, after his deepest loneliness has been taken up in walking with God, may be due to the lack of human intercourse; and the burden, the stuffiness, the weariness in her experience, after the need of others and her own need of their need has been recognized, may be due to the lack of solitude. The total life, that is, may be possible, may exist, and it may answer to every quest.

To find the total life, it seems, would be to find God. "He does not perceive separated lives and actions more clearly than the total life," Yeats says of the man who finds God, "for the total life has suddenly displayed its source." It would mean letting God be his whole life. "His joy is to be nothing, to do nothing, to think nothing," Yeats says, "but to permit the total life, expressed in its humanity, to flow in upon him and to express itself through his acts and thoughts."[11] The man we are imagining has already found God in solitude, but God has not yet become his whole life. He has yet to find God in the human circle. If he does find God there, we can expect, it will be to him a dark God. It will be like the woman finding God in solitude, to her a dark God, seen under the image of the night sky, felt within as the "water of night."

2. THE BRIGHT GOD AND THE DARK GOD

"God has a terrible double aspect," Jung says in his *Answer to Job*, "a sea of grace is met by a seething lake of fire, and the light of love glows with a fierce dark heat of which it is said 'ardet non lucet'—it burns but gives no light."[12] The double aspect of God appears, it seems, when one enters upon an unknown life, as we are envisioning, when one comes from the human circle into solitude, when one comes from solitude into the human circle. It is not that God is actually double, we could say perhaps in contrast to Jung's understanding of the matter, but that there is an ambiguity in human feeling toward the unknown life, a double feeling of dread and fascination. "That is the eternal, as distinct from the temporal, gospel," Jung goes on to say; "*one can love God but must fear him.*"[13] When one comes from the human circle into solitude, like the woman we are imagining, one can love the God one finds in solitude but one must fear him, simply because one loves and fears the unknown life, though one can overcome the fear— "After so many years of mad, aimless fleeing from fear, she had come to a stop at last." Likewise when one comes from solitude into the human circle, like the man we are imagining, one can love God, for one knows from one's experience in solitude that "the love is from God and of God and towards God," but one must fear God, for one knows that the loneliness one left behind in the human circle and that originally drove one out of the human circle is also "from God and of God and towards God."

Is the love of God only a "temporal gospel" and is the love and fear an "eternal gospel"? No, it seems there is a resolving of the double aspect of God into a oneness, like resolving a double image in optics, like focusing. It occurs when one finds the total life, when one "does not perceive separated lives and actions more clearly than the total life, for the total life has suddenly displayed its source." There is the testimony of experience to a love that casts out fear. "There is no fear in love," according to the First Epistle of John—and we can suppose this is a testimony of experience—"but perfect love casts out fear."[14]

Let us see how the brightness and darkness of God will appear to one coming into solitude and to one coming into the human circle, how "a sea of grace is met by a seething lake of fire, and the light of love glows with a fierce dark heat." Let us see if we can find the way of resolving the double image, of focusing it into a single image, of passing from the split between the known and the unknown life into the wholeness of the total life.

What does one fear of God in solitude? Or better, what do we fear in solitude when we hide from it in the human circle?

It is like the child's fear of the dark. Camus describes it when he tells about the "Adulterous Woman" with her husband before she goes out into solitude:

They made love in the dark by feel, without seeing each other. Is there another love than that of darkness, a love that would cry aloud in daylight? She didn't know, but she did know that he needed her and that she needed that need, that she lived on it night and day, at night especially—every night, when he didn't want to be alone, or to age or die, with that set expression he assumed which she occasionally recognized on other men's faces, the only common expression of those madmen hiding under an appearance of wisdom until the madness seizes them and hurls them desperately towards a woman's body to bury in it, without desire, everything terrifying that solitude and night reveals to them.[15]

It is the fear of being alone, or aging, of dying. It is the fear of night and of everything the darkness of night contains. To go out into solitude, to go out into the desert night as the woman in this story does, is to meet the fear head-on. It is to make love with what one fears. It is to let it make love. It is to enter into a love that casts out fear.

What then does one fear of God in the human circle? Or, what do we fear in the human circle when we hide from it in solitude? It is a fear of going back to the fear we knew in the human circle. It is a fear of fear. It is a fear of being in need like the husband of the "Adulterous Woman" or of being in need of need like the woman herself. There is need in the love of man and woman, but there is also need in work and in communal life. There is in each of them the need of other persons and the need to be needed by other persons. To be living in such need is to be living in fear, and once we have escaped from it into solitude we are reluctant to go back to it, afraid to go back to it. The need reflects the loneliness that surrounds love and work and communal life. The original fear of solitude arose out of loneliness and made us "madmen" whose "madness seizes them and hurls them desperately towards a woman's body to bury in it, without desire, everything terrifying that solitude and night reveals to them." Once we have escaped from the loneliness into the love that one can find in solitude, we fear to return to the human circle, for we fear the loneliness, we fear the madness. We fear it all the more because we know that in spite of the love there is something of the loneliness still with us. We know we are liable to the loneliness.

"Is there another love than that of darkness, a love that would cry aloud in daylight?" "That of darkness" is what we are calling "the loneliness." It is what holds the husband of the "Adulterous Woman" in the human circle, burying in her body everything that terrifies him about solitude. It is what leads the woman herself out into solitude; certainly it is what has led the man we have been imagining out into solitude, longing for a communion that cannot be found in the human circle. There in solitude the woman makes love with the night sky, and the man we have been imagining finds a love that is "from God and of God and towards God." There we have "another love than that of darkness," but it is not yet the love that Camus is asking about, for he is thinking of a love of man and woman. If one were to come back with the love one finds in solitude, if one were to bring it with one into the human circle, would it become there "a love that would cry aloud in daylight"?

At every stage the question is that of the loneliness. The loneliness can hold one in the human circle; it can drive one into solitude; and it can deter one from returning to the human circle. Insofar as the loneliness is "from God and of God and towards God" it is the dark side of God. Or, to speak more accurately, it is the human experience of the dark side of God. When one is hiding in the human circle from "everything terrifying that solitude and night reveals," one is hiding, as it seems to one, from a dark God. One may be like Mark Twain, a believer at night, a skeptic during the day.[16] The loneliness may drive one "towards God" by inspiring one to fear God, and it may seem "from God" in that the fear seizes one like a madness. At the same time it may lead one to interpose another human being between oneself and God, to love another human being with the dark love that is fear of night and of solitude. It may lead one more generally to "take refuge in humanity,"[17] as Camus says, to surround oneself with other human beings, to try and shield oneself with love and work and communal life.

If one abandons one's refuge in humanity, if one leaves the human circle and goes out into solitude, one is responding to the desire rather than the fear in the loneliness. One is following out the heart's desire for an intimacy deeper than any one has found in the human circle. The God one meets then in solitude is both bright and dark, like the night sky, bright with stars and yet dark with night. The bright side of God is the love that is "from God and of God and towards God"; the dark side is the loneliness out of which the love arises. Why isn't the loneliness totally consumed in the love? Perhaps because in going into solitude one has left a great deal of one's life behind, one's life in the human circle, and so the love is not yet able to be one's whole life. At any rate, the experience in solitude is not always that of love, of powerful longing, but at some moments is that of loneliness, of weak and ineffectual longing. At those moments the solitary man is solitary again, and he is tempted by the fear and the desire of all that is missing from his life. It is like *The Temptation of Saint Anthony*, the novel of Flaubert inspired by the painting of Breughel, a nightmare of dread and fascination. The dark side of God appears to him in those moments not as God but as what is not God. It seems that God is not enough for him. It is not apparent to him in those moments that the loneliness is "from God and of God and towards God."

When one returns, therefore, from solitude to the human circle, there is a double meaning in what one is doing. One is returning to share with others what one has found, but one is also seeking to find in the human circle what one has not found in solitude. The sharing comes out of the experience of the bright side of God. It is a sharing of the love, and it may indeed become in the human circle "a love that would cry aloud in daylight," a love that would express itself in love and work and communal life. The seeking, however, comes out of the experience of the dark side of God. It is the dark love one left behind in the human circle, a love that is full of the fear of being alone. One feels it and fears it. One is drawn by it toward the human circle but at the same time repelled by it and deterred from entering the human circle. On account of it the human circle itself draws one and repels one. Insight comes when one sees that the dark love is indeed a loneliness that is "from God and of God and towards God," that one is actually seeking God in the human circle.

Then it becomes apparent that the goal is a marriage of God and the soul. It becomes apparent, too, that the marriage has to be consummated in the darkness of the dark side of God. One has to find God, that is, in the loneliness that is "from God and of God and towards God." The thing one fears about solitude is aloneness; the thing one fears about the human circle is need. The loneliness is the experience of both the aloneness and the need. One has to go through both the aloneness and the need, it seems, if the loneliness is to be consummated fully in love. One has to go through "the night in

Gethsemane when the last friends have fallen asleep," Dag Hammarskjöld says, "all others are seeking your downfall, and *God is silent*, as the marriage is consummated."[18]

It is in "the dark night of the soul," according to Saint John of the Cross, that the marriage of God and the soul takes place. We can interpret "the dark night of the soul," it seems, as the experience of going through the loneliness that is "from God and of God and towards God." There are in fact two nights, according to Saint John, a "night of sense" and a "night of spirit."[19] We can connect the "night of sense," it seems, with the experience of Jesus going out into the desert. There is in going out into the desert an experience of deprivation of the senses in giving oneself over to the life of the spirit. "Man shall not live by bread alone," he says at that time, "but by every word that proceeds from the mouth of God."[20] We can connect the "night of spirit," on the other hand, with the experience of Jesus in Gethsemane, "My Father, if it be possible, let this cup pass from me; nevertheless, not as I will, but as thou wilt," and with his experience on Calvary, "My God, my God, why hast thou forsaken me?"[21] The "night of sense" seems to occur in what we have been describing as the journey into solitude, while the "night of spirit" seems to occur at the end of the journey back again from solitude into the human circle.

There is a union with God that takes place already in solitude. It is an entering into a to-and-fro with God. The man we have been imagining went out into solitude and entered there into a to-and-fro with God, and in "the heart's vision" this turned out to be a to-and-fro within God himself, as in the Christian doctrine of the Trinity. He saw himself entering into the eternal relationship of the Father and the Son. That was a union of God and the self. Now, as he returns to the human circle, he seems to be moving toward another kind of union with God, a union of God and the soul. The marriage of God and the soul, according to Saint John of the Cross, takes place in the "night of spirit." As we are envisioning it, this is to come about in the human circle. The woman in Camus' story entered into a kind of divine marriage in solitude. For her the unknown life, the life of the soul, was that of solitude; for the man we have been envisioning, however, it is that of the human circle. The marriage of God and the soul thus seems always to take place in the darkness of the unknown life. The remarkable thing about the "dark night of the soul" is that in spite of all the darkness it is, according to Saint John, a "happy night."[22] The experience that takes place in the darkness of the dark side of God, whether it be in solitude or in the human circle, is in the end a happy experience.

3. THE QUEST OF SOUL

"If I could overcome that fear," the woman says to herself in Camus' story, "I'd be happy."[23] She says this before she goes out into the unknown. She is speaking of the fear of death. The fear of the unknown life is a fear of death, for the unknown life is seen as the end of the life one knows. The woman here sees the life of solitude as the end of the life she knows in the human circle. The man we are imagining, on the other hand, sees the life of the human circle as the end of the life he knows in solitude. The known life and the unknown life, the life of self and the life of soul, we could say, are related to one another as life and death. We could say of self and soul what Heraclitus says of the elements or what he says of mortals and immortals: "They live one another's death and die one another's life."[24] As we shall see, there is a story implicit in this: soul lives the death of self and dies the life of self, and self lives the death of soul and dies the life of soul.

We began this chapter by seeing in the unknown life the

prospect of love. Now we are seeing in it the prospect of death. We were speaking when we began from the standpoint of desire. Now we are speaking from the standpoint of fear. The man we are imagining, nevertheless, could say what the woman says: "If I could overcome that fear, I'd be happy." If he could overcome that fear, he could go out into the unknown—for him the human circle; he could enter into the unknown life—for him a life of relatedness with other human beings. He would be happy, it seems, not simply because of the relatedness with other human beings—others have that and are not happy—but because he will have entered into the unknown life, because his soul will have come to life, because God will have become not only the life of his self but also the life of his soul.

There is love in the unknown life, and there is death too, simply because the unknown life carries one beyond the life of self. It remains to be seen what love there is and what death there is. Let us suppose the man we are envisioning does overcome his fear and does go out into the unknown realm of the human circle. Let us suppose he does enter into the unknown life of relatedness with other human beings. Let us see what love he will find, and what death, and what happiness.

"A new life begins,"[25] Dante says when he meets Beatrice. That is a clue for us as to what love the man we are envisioning will find and also what death he will find and what happiness. We can connect what Dante calls "the new life" with what we have been calling "the unknown life." Dante sees a mysterious life in Beatrice, an unknown life, a new life, and he is drawn to her. He is inspired to pursue that life, to live it himself. This kindling of his heart is substantially what happens between him and her. There is no developed human relationship between them with all the ins and outs that are experienced when two persons live in close touch with each other over a considerable length of time. He only sees her a few times. She smiles at him. Then she dies and he is left without her. All he has then is memory, the memory of her, the memory of the moment of exaltation when he saw the new life in her, the memory of the terrible moment when death took her away from him, and the memory of the new life itself embodied in her but still possible for him even after her death.

We can imagine something similar happening between the man and the woman we are envisioning, even without supposing that the woman actually dies. It is what happens whenever one person finds in another a new and unknown life: each sees in the other a mysterious life, and each is drawn to the other in the hope of sharing the other's life. Yet there is death between them, for the new life each sees in the other is like death to the life that is familiar. "They live one another's death and die one another's life." They enter into a friendship, but their friendship is not based on sharing a life that is familiar, like that of two persons who live within the human circle, who live within the same world. Rather, it is based on sharing an unknown life. Each is linked through the other to an unknown world, to a life beyond the familiar, to a life that seems to lie on the other side of death.

When one discovers a new life in another person, one begins to carry within one an image of the other, like Dante carrying within him the image of Beatrice and, after her death, the memory of Beatrice. Jung has it that man carries within him an image of woman, the *anima* or "soul," and woman carries within her an image of man, the *animus* or "spirit."[26] As Jung understands it, however, the image is already there before one meets the other, and when the meeting actually occurs the image lends the meeting its significance. "Other people are established inalienably in my memories," he writes in the prologue to his autobiography, "only if their names were entered in the scrolls of my destiny from the beginning, so that encountering them was at the same time a kind of recollection."[27]

Another way of understanding the matter is to see in the meeting of one person and another, as we are seeing, the actual discovery of a new and unknown life. The image of the other, if we understand it this way, arises out of the discovery. What Dante means by "a new life," what Proust means by "an unknown life," it seems, is a life that is actually discovered in the other person. It is a life to which the other actually does link one. No doubt, the life one finds in the other is a life that one lacks, and the image one forms of the other reaches beyond the life the other person actually lives. The man we are imagining, for instance, sees in the woman the possibility of a relationship untainted by need, and she sees in him the possibility of a solitude untainted by loneliness. One brings to the meeting with the other one's own lack, and the image one forms of the other is one of fulfillment. Still one comes to understand one's lack only in coming to know the other, and the other does open up the way to fulfillment. When one meets the other, one has an experience not of recollection so much as of something being inscribed upon one's memory. In "the book of my memory," Dante says, speaking of his meeting with Beatrice, are inscribed the words "a new life begins."[28]

In fact, the image one forms of the other is not only an image of life but also an image of death. "Death," Rilke says, "is the side of life that is turned away from, and unillumined by, us."[29] What he says of death we could say of the new and unknown life, the life of soul. It is "the side of life that is turned away from, and unillumined by, us." We can see death —actual death, that is—under the image of a new and unknown life, and vice versa we can see a new and unknown life under the image of death. If the person in whom one discovers a new life dies, like Beatrice, then one may begin to see death itself under the image of the new life, and the person in whom one discovered the new life may become, like Beatrice for Dante, one's link to the life beyond death, one's link to the otherworld. Even if the other person does not die, though, one may see the new life under the image of death, for it is the end of the life one knows, the end of the world one knows. If the other person dies, the road of one's quest seems to lead into the kingdom of death, like that of Dante seeking Beatrice or that of Orpheus seeking Eurydice. Even if the other person does not die, one has the uneasy feeling that one must somehow pass through death in order to actually live the new life.

As long as another person is one's only link to a new and unknown life, one does not yet live the new life oneself. As long as another person is the link, the other mediates the new life to one, stands between one and the new life, joins one to it and also separates one from it. If one loses the other person, if the other dies, if the other is estranged, then one loses one's connection with the new life unless one can find the other again, or find someone else to link one to it, or at last come actually to live the new life oneself. The "marriage of God and the soul," it seems, would mean just that, living the new and unknown life oneself, as the marriage of man and woman could mean being linked to the new and unknown life through another human being.

When the new life is that of solitude, as it is for the woman we are envisioning, then it is clear that one is not living the new life oneself as long as one's only link to it is another person. When the new life is that of the human circle, on the other hand, as it is for the man, then it is not so clear. It can seem to him that he is already living the life of the human circle simply through his friendship with the woman. In reality, the friendship of the man and the woman we are envisioning is based, as we have seen, on sharing an unknown life. It is essentially different from a friendship based on sharing a life that is familiar to both, a friendship within the human circle. Rather, it is a mediating friendship. Each mediates between the other and a life that is new and unknown to the other. There is a tension in it that does not exist in a simple friendship within the human circle. Each person has a journey still to travel, the man a journey into the human circle, the woman a journey into solitude.

Each has a death to undergo, passing over into the other side of life, but each hopes to come thereby into a total life that can be fully shared with the other, a life that courses through two worlds, the world of solitude and the world of the human circle. It is like the life Rilke says he is describing in his *Duino Elegies*, a life that lives on both sides of death:

Affirmation of life as well as of death prove themselves one in the *Elegies*. To admit the one without the other would, it is here realised with exultance, be a limitation which would ultimately exclude everything infinite. Death is the side of life that is turned away from, and unillumined by, us: we must try to achieve the greatest possible consciousness of our being, which is at home in both these immeasurable realms and is nourished inexhaustibly by both. The true pattern of life extends through both domains, the blood with the greatest circuit runs through both: there is neither a This-side nor a That-side but a single great unity in which the beings who transcend us, the angels, have their habitation.[30]

A life that lives in both worlds, that of solitude and that of the human circle, appears indeed to live on both sides of death. If one lives in the human circle, death appears under the image of solitude. Death singles one out; one has to die while the others go on living. If one lives in solitude, on the other hand, death appears under the image of the human circle. One has to rejoin mankind in death; one has to undergo the common fate of all human beings. If one passes, therefore, from the human circle into solitude, one goes out into the realm of death while others go on living in the human circle, one is singled out and yet one still lives. Likewise, if one passes from solitude into the human circle, one joins mankind in death, one submits to the common fate of all human beings and yet one still lives. Either way, one passes into another world, and to that extent one dies, and yet one survives death. One discovers then that "the true pattern of life extends through both domains" and "the blood with the greatest circuit runs through both," both life and death, as Rilke is saying, both solitude and the human circle, as we are saying, for one of the two worlds will be the very image of life and the other will be the very image of death.

"The road up and down is one and the same,"[31] Heraclitus says. The way into solitude and into the human circle, we could say too, is one and the same. One travels it in one direction, going into solitude, and one travels it in the other, going into the human circle. Whichever direction one takes, it seems from what we have found so far, the way leads through the loneliness of the human condition. There is a longing in that loneliness, and that is what leads one to travel at all. There is the experience of aloneness, and there is the experience of need. If one is unwilling to be alone, one dwells in the human circle like many an ordinary person. If one is unwilling to be in need, one dwells in solitude like many a solitary individual. But if one is willing to walk alone and willing to be in need, one travels the way. The willingness to walk alone enables one to take the way into solitude; the willingness to be in need enables one to take the way into the human circle. There is a paradox here. If one is willing to walk alone, we have found, one does not have to walk alone after all, but one finds God in solitude and comes to walk with God. If one is willing to be in need, we can ask now, does one find God in the human circle and does God fulfill one's need?

Willingness to walk alone, it is true, is not the same as resignation to being alone. On the contrary, we have envisioned a man who went out into solitude, willing to walk alone and yet hoping to be unalone. It was this combination of willingness to walk alone and hope of being unalone, it seems, that enabled him to find God in solitude. So too willingness to be in need is not the same as resignation to being unfulfilled. We can envision him now coming from solitude into the human circle, willing to be in need and yet hoping for fulfillment. It is like a person on his deathbed who is willing to die and yet hopes to live. Oftentimes, it is said, such a person experiences a remission of the fatal disease and recovers his health.

Before the remission occurs, nevertheless, he does go through a period of fatal sickness, a sickness that brings him to his deathbed. The man we have been imagining may have to go through such a period too, a period of loss of soul, a period like the one Dante went through after losing Beatrice. For in accepting need one becomes liable to suffering losses one would not suffer if one held to the autonomy one can enjoy in solitude. One comes to need the person who links one to the new life, and one becomes liable to losing that person and losing one's link and losing touch with the new life. One may have to go through and beyond loss to live the new life oneself. "Unless one hopes," Heraclitus says, "one will not find the unhoped-for."[32] When one finds a new life in another person, one begins to hope. When one loses the other person, one's hopes seem dashed. It is then that one may hope to find the "unhoped-for."

6

Loss of Soul

"THE mass of men lead lives of quiet desperation."[1] Thoreau says that at the beginning of *Walden* when he is about to describe his own withdrawal into solitude. There is a quiet desperation that one leaves behind when one goes out into solitude in quest of a deeper life. It is a desperation that comes from the lack of any great hope, the lack of any great thing to live for. When one goes out into solitude, one leaves it behind in the hope of finding and living a deeper life.

When one comes back again to the human circle, one brings with one the deeper life one has found in solitude, and yet one may find oneself facing once again a life of quiet desperation. One finds a deeper life in solitude, but it does not become one's whole life. It cannot be one's whole life until one finds it also in the human circle. When one comes back to the human circle, one sees how far one is from living it to the full. There are parts of one's being that have not yet been touched by the deeper life, parts that have to do with one's need of other persons and one's need to be needed by others. These parts have remained unkindled and unillumined in the midst of all the kindling and illumining that have taken place in solitude. There is still a quiet desperation about these needs, for one has not yet found a hope of fulfilling them. To come to such a hope one may have to let oneself feel one's needs and one's own share in the quiet desperation of mankind. One may have to go through need and quiet desperation to hope and a deeper life much as one might go through sorrow to joy.

It is possible to have a need without letting oneself feel it. An unfelt need like this is what Freud calls an "affect."[2] It appears as a need in the pattern of one's behavior and can often be perceived by another person even though one does not perceive it very well oneself. If one does let oneself feel such a need, then the affect becomes feeling, and that can be a painful process. It is analogous to what happens when one's arm or leg is numb and sensation begins to return. There is pain at first, but when sensation has returned fully there is a sense of well-being. Let us see what it would be to let oneself feel the quiet desperation of one's needs. Let us see what it would be to pass from numbness through pain to well-being in the human circle.

1. "HE WHO FINDS HIS SOUL WILL LOSE IT"

One discovers one's needs in the human circle when one finds a new life in another person, as Dante did in Beatrice. The pain comes when one falls into the fear of losing or, like Dante, into the despair of having lost the person who embodies the new life. To lose the other, it seems then, is to lose one's soul. As we have been using the terms, the life of "self" is the life with which one is familiar, while the life of "soul" is the mysterious life one finds in the world of the other person. When one meets the other, "a new life begins," as Dante says, one finds "an unknown life," as Proust says. If one loses the other person after having found life in the other, however, one is left to one's own devices, one is left to find life for oneself. Dante, after he has lost Beatrice, begins to speak of his "first love," Beatrice, and his "second love," philosophy.[3] He seeks to make his own way into the unknown world she has opened up for him. It is only after this effort of "self" has failed that he comes back again to "soul." He brings his two loves together in one quest. He finds Beatrice again, though she is dead, and she becomes his guide in the unknown world.

There is a saying of Jesus where these ironic turns of event seem to be anticipated: "He who finds his life will lose it, and he who loses his life for my sake will find it."[4] The word that is being translated "life" here is actually *psyche*, the word for "soul." No doubt "life" is the correct translation, and the saying is not differentiating life, as we are, into that of "self" and that of "soul." Still, if we translate "soul," the saying formulates the very pattern of events we are finding in experience and in the life of Dante: "He who finds his soul will lose it, and he who loses his soul for my sake will find it." There is a finding and a losing, and there is a losing and a finding. The saying does not envision these as a continuous sequence of events but as alternative paths, on one of them one finds and loses, on the other one loses and finds. We can imagine a person going like Dante, though, from one path to the other, first finding and losing, then losing and finding. Such a person would know the truth of the saying from his own experience.

Say the man we have been envisioning goes through this entire pattern of events, finding and losing and then losing and finding. Why does one who finds "a new life" lose it? And why does one who loses it "for my sake" find it?

If I find "a new life" in another person and then lose that person, I may well ask myself these questions, hoping to find a way of regaining the person or at least of regaining the life.

Kierkegaard, for instance, asked himself questions like these
after he had lost Regina. He loved Regina and lost her, hoped
to regain her, but succeeded only in coming to himself. While
he was still hoping to regain her, he formulated a theory according to which one receives back from God what one has
willingly given up in faith, like Abraham receiving back Isaac.
But then it seemed to him, when he failed to regain Regina and
succeeded only in coming to himself, that the thing one loses is
oneself and it is oneself that one regains.[5] Thus selfhood became the central notion in Kierkegaard's thinking, and he
came to understand the finding and the losing in terms of selfhood, as if to say, "He who finds himself will lose himself, and
he who loses himself for my sake will find himself."

There are really two patterns of experience, therefore, that
we have to consider: that of Dante and Beatrice and that of
Kierkegaard and Regina. Dante meets Beatrice, then he loses
her through death, and then he finds her again somehow on the
other side of death. Kierkegaard meets Regina, then he loses
her through estrangement, but he does not find her again on
the other side of estrangement. He finds only himself. The self
he comes to, it is true, is a self grounded in God. "By relating
itself to its own self, and by willing to be itself," he says, "the
self is grounded transparently in the Power which constituted
it."[6] That is his definition of the condition in which there is no
despair. It seems like the love the man we have been imagining
has come to in solitude, a love in which God is the life of the
self. Dante, though, seems to come to something more. He
finds the new life and then he loses it, but when he finds Beatrice again he finds the new life once again and he becomes
caught up, as he says, in "the love that moves the sun and the
other stars."[7] That seems like the love toward which the man
we are imagining is now moving, a love in which God is the
life of the soul.

A period of loss occurs, even a period of despair and desperation, in both patterns of experience. There are moments of despair in *The New Life* where Dante tells how he met Beatrice and then lost her. There is a kind of desperation in *The Banquet* where he tries to replace Beatrice, his "first love," with philosophy, his "second love." Then there is a going through and beyond despair and desperation in *The Divine Comedy* where he goes through hell and purgatory to paradise, finds Beatrice again, and is caught up in "the love that moves the sun and the other stars." There is a comparable sequence of events in Kierkegaard's works from *Repetition* where he tells of the despair he went through at the loss of Regina and of his coming to himself to *Sickness unto Death* where he gives a universal rendering of his experience and tells how universally a human being must go through and beyond despair in order to come to the condition in which "the self is grounded transparently in the Power which constituted it."

Despair, when it comes from losing a person one loves, can go with a state of being unable to forget the loved one. If one could only despair completely, one thinks, one could forget. But the desire for the other keeps creating a hope of reunion, and the real situation keeps destroying that hope. So one finds oneself plunged into despair not once but over and over again. One hopes again every day and despairs again every day. The full cycle is desire=hope=disappointment=despair. One can try to break the cycle by not letting oneself despair, by not letting oneself be disappointed, by not letting oneself hope, by not letting oneself even desire, but none of these measures seem to work except as forms of self-deception. In reality one does desire, one does hope, and one is disappointed, and one does despair.

Desperation then becomes a way out of despair and out of the cycle of despair. It is the attempt to find a replacement for what one has lost. One may try to replace the person one has lost with another person, like Dante in his period of desperation trying to replace Beatrice with other women; or one may try to replace one's love for the person with love for the unknown world into which the person has led one, like Dante trying to go from Beatrice, his "first love," to philosophy, his "second love." One may try both at once, like Dante, and feel within oneself the split between body and mind, between the passions of the body and the passions of the mind. The split itself is the sign of one's failure and can plunge one back into despair and the cycle of despair. Yet it can be at the same time a sign of what is missing, of what has been lost, namely the life of the soul. It is as though the life of the soul is the middle ground between the life of the body and the life of the mind, as though self without soul is divided between body and mind. To suffer through the conflict of one's passions, to suffer through the split between body and mind may be the way to recovery.

If we keep silence about soul and speak only of self, what we are saying about despair and desperation becomes similar to Kierkegaard's approach to his despair at losing Regina. Despair, as he understands it in *Sickness unto Death*, is always despair over oneself. It ranges from not even knowing that one has a self, the condition one is in before one loses the other, to knowing but being unwilling to be oneself, the condition one is in after one loses the other and sees oneself naked and alone, to willing despairingly to be oneself, the condition one gets into by trying to save oneself without God. Despair is overcome, Kierkegaard believes, when one takes the final step, from will to willingness, from a will to be oneself to a willingness to be oneself, receiving oneself from God as a gift.

When Kierkegaard describes despair over oneself, it seems he is actually describing the condition of the self without soul, a self that is indeed in despair. If we take soul into account, we seem to gain a further insight into each stage. The first is one of quiet desperation. It is like the condition Thoreau is speaking of when he says "The mass of men lead lives of quiet desperation." It comes to an end when one can say, as Dante does when he meets Beatrice, "a new life begins." The second stage, being unwilling to be oneself, comes about when one passes from "a new life begins" to "a new life ends," when one goes through the experience of loss. The self one is unwilling to be, it seems, is the self one is without the other person one has lost, the self without soul. It is the same as the self of quiet desperation except that now it has become conscious of its lack of soul. The third stage, willing despairingly to be oneself, is not a will to be this self without soul, it seems, but a will to find one's soul and to be the self endowed with the new and unknown life. At this stage one has passed, in our terms, from "despair" to "desperation," active now rather than quiet desperation. Hope is only a hairsbreadth away. The change comes when one passes from will to willingness, to be endowed with soul, to live the new and unknown life.

At each stage the total life of self and soul is at stake. Quiet desperation, despair, and active desperation are stages in a journey through hell. While one is going through them one could well see oneself as living in a hell. What is happening, though, in all this dark journey is that the self is becoming capable of soul. Living without the life of soul, then finding it in another person and losing it, and then seeking desperately to regain it, one is becoming capable of actually living it. The crucial step is the final one, from will to willingness. As Kierkegaard conceives it, the step is from a will to be oneself to a willingness to be oneself, or, in his terms, from "willing despairingly" to be oneself to willing to be oneself "grounded" in God. As we are conceiving it, the step is from a will to live the new and unknown life to a willingness to live it, from a quest

like Dante's "second love" to a quest like his journey through
the otherworld, from a will to make one's soul, as in Yeats'
line "Now shall I make my soul,"[8] to a willingness to receive
one's soul, to let God be the life of one's soul.

Between Dante and Kierkegaard something seems to have
happened in the history of self and soul. There has been an
historic loss of soul, it seems, and an historic emergence of self.
Kierkegaard fell back on self because of what happened in his
own life, we may say, because he lost Regina and did not
regain her; but he was able to fall back on self, we may guess,
because of an historic emergence of self, because self had become important enough by his time to make it appear that a
human being is essentially a self. As he defines it, "the self is a
relation which relates itself to its own self,"[9] but it relates itself
to its own self rather than to the other, it relates to itself in
losing the other, it falls back upon itself, and so it is equivalent
to what we are calling "self" in contrast with "soul." The
emergence of the self in history seems to be part of the emergence of the individual. There is first the emergence of mankind, we were saying earlier, and then the emergence of the
individual. Yet the self without soul is an individual who is
diminished. There has been a loss on the scale of history, it
seems, like the loss that occurred in the lives of Dante and
Kierkegaard. There has been a bereavement, an encounter
with death, that has left the emerging individual bereft of soul.

2. SELF WITHOUT SOUL

A few years after Dante died Europe was devastated by the
plague. The experience of the Black Death, as it was called,
seems to have brought about a change in the consciousness of
death in Western culture.[10] Before the time of the Black
Death there was a feeling that death was part of life. It had

been possible for Dante to live on both sides of death, to go on an imaginative journey into the otherworld to find Beatrice. After the Black Death a new feeling developed of death as something external to life, something breaking in upon life from the outside and destroying it. One can see the new feeling emerging in the Dance of Death, as it was represented and performed in the fourteenth, fifteenth, and sixteenth centuries, and one can see the growing fear of death in the poetry of the seventeenth century, the fear that one will perish in death, that death will be the utter end:

> I have a sinne of feare, that when I have spunne
> My last thred, I shall perish on the shore;
> Sweare by thy selfe, that at my death thy Sunne
> Shall shine as it shines now, and heretofore;
> And, having done that, Thou hast done,
> I have no more. [11]

Here the fear of perishing is balanced, as elsewhere in Donne's poetry, by hope, but in the eighteenth and nineteenth centuries the fear deepens into despair. It is despair over oneself in the face of death that Kierkegaard is wrestling with in *Sickness unto Death*. He, too, comes to hope, but he has to pass not only through fear but also through despair to reach it.

What has happened, it seems, is that man has been reduced to himself by the prospect of death. There are two great certainties about the self: "I am" and "I will die."[12] When death is set over against life, when it is seen as something breaking in upon life from the outside and destroying it, then the certainty that "I will die" is set over against the certainty that "I am." If the certainty that "I am" can be associated with mind, as in Descartes' saying "I think therefore I am,"[13] the certainty that "I will die" can be associated with body, with the mortality of the human body. Indeed mind and body are set over against one another in Descartes' thinking,[14] and not only in his thinking, it seems, but in the actual experience of being reduced to oneself by the prospect of death. There is a fear in being reduced to oneself, and there is a loneliness, and there is a dividedness of self against other, mind against body, "I am" against "I will die."

It is the clash between "I am" and "I will die," it seems, that is being felt in the fear, the loneliness, the dividedness. One can feel it even if one has not gone through a personal loss like Dante or Kierkegaard. It is an historic condition. How is one to pass from "I am" and "I will die" into a life that lives on both sides of death?

There is a clue for us in Cocteau's *Orpheus* where the entrance to the otherworld is a mirror. Eurydice dies and Orpheus goes into the otherworld to find her, and he is allowed to bring her back with him on condition that he not look around at her, but he does look and she vanishes among the shades. That much is in the traditional story, but Cocteau adds a mirror. He has Death come through a mirror to take Eurydice away, then he has Orpheus follow them through the mirror into the otherworld, and then he has Orpheus and Eurydice come back again through the mirror into this world. "Mirrors are doors," he has an angel tell Orpheus. "It's through them that Death moves back and forth into life." "Besides," he adds, "spend your life looking at yourself in a mirror, and you'll see Death at work like a swarm of bees storing up honey in a hive of glass."[15]

What one sees in a mirror is oneself, but the self who says "I am" sees in the mirror the self who says "I will die," sees "Death at work like a swarm of bees storing up honey in a hive of glass." The glass seems to separate the self who says "I will die" from the self who says "I am." If Orpheus steps into the mirror, he can find Eurydice again; if the self who says "I am" steps into the self who says "I will die," if one steps into one's mortal image in the mirror, one can find one's soul. Dante calls the memory of Beatrice his "soul."[16] He also calls her "the life of my heart."[17] For she embodies for him the new life and links him to it. Eurydice is the soul of Orpheus, we could say, as Beatrice is the soul of Dante and Regina is the soul of Kierkegaard. When there is a split between "I am" and "I will die," we could say too, there has been a loss of soul, like the loss of Eurydice. Soul is the missing link between the self who says, "I am" and the self who says, "I will die."

If we compare Descartes' "three substances"[18]—God and mind and body—with the earlier tradition going back to Plotinus of "four substances"[19]—God and mind and soul and body—we can see that something has dropped out in early modern thought, namely soul. It has dropped out between mind and body, between "I am" and "I will die." It has left the modern person in the stance of "I am" looking in the mirror at "I will die":

How well I understand the mirror symbolism in Cocteau's *Orphée*. To break through the barrier which, when I encounter reality, prevents my encountering myself—to break through it, even at the price of having to enter the Kingdom of Death. Nevertheless —what do I long for more ardently than just this? When and how shall I find the occasion to do it? Or is it already too late? Is my contact with others anything more than a contact with reflections? Who or what can give me the power to transform the mirror into a doorway?[20]

Dag Hammarskjöld records these reflections in his diary just before the great turning point of his life when, as he put it afterward, "I did answer *Yes* to Someone—or Something."[21] That *Yes* and that "Someone—or Something" was the answer, it seems, to the questions he poses here, especially the last one,

"Who or what can give me the power to transform the mirror into a doorway?" One answer to that last question would be to say that the "who" for Orpheus is Eurydice, for Dante is Beatrice, for Kierkegaard is Regina, and the "what" is the new and unknown life, that one passes through the mirror when one says *Yes* to the person who embodies the new and unknown life and *Yes* to the life itself. That would be an answer for someone who finds himself in our historic situation of self without soul and has found a person who embodies for him the life of soul, who can become for him what Dante calls Beatrice, "the life of my heart." For someone like the man we have been imagining, however, who has lost that very person, who has fallen like Dante or Kierkegaard under the saying "He who finds his soul will lose it," that is no longer an answer.

Another answer would be to say that the "who" is oneself and the "what" is death, that one passes through the mirror when one says *Yes* to oneself, both to the self who says "I am" and to the self who says "I will die," so that the two become one and the same self. That would be a development of Kierkegaard's *Yes* to the self who says "I am." It would extend the *Yes* to the self who says "I will die." If one were to do that, one will have stepped into one's mortal image in the mirror, one will have entered like Orpheus into the otherworld, but one will still have the task of finding Eurydice.

Say the man we have been imagining makes that move, says *Yes* to "I am" and "I will die." Those have always been the two great certainties of his life. He has lived in the one, "I am," and has been surrounded by the other, "I will die," encountering it in every direction he turns, as if he were living in a hall of mirrors. Now that he accepts it and takes it into himself, steps into it and begins to live in it, he is no longer surrounded by it. Instead he is surrounded by uncertainty. Until now his vision of his life has been a vision of aloneness, a vision of an

individual living and dying by himself. Now he sees that there
has been a blind spot in his vision. He is certain that he will
die, and his vision of walking alone goes somehow with that
certainty. He is uncertain, though, as to what death he will die,
and he is uncertain too, and for the same reason, as to what
life he will live. The two go together, the life he will live and
the death he will die. He is certain only *that* he lives and *that*
he will die, and he is certain of being alone only in that it is *he*
who lives and *he* who will die. Beyond that he is uncertain, and
there is room in that uncertainty for a life together.

To cling to his aloneness, he sees, would be to cling to his
certainty and flee from his uncertainty. To enter his uncertainty, on the other hand, would be to enter the human circle
of love and work and communal life. It is an insight for him to
see the connection between the human circle and his own
inner uncertainty. For he has been living a very inward life, as
we have been describing it, and now he doesn't know how to
make an outward move until he knows the inward move that
goes with it. The outward move is entering the human circle.
The inward move is entering his uncertainty. To enter his uncertainty is to become conscious of it and willing to live in it.
As his uncertainty becomes conscious it becomes a seeing. As
it becomes willing it becomes a choosing. He sees our life together and he chooses it.

If one lives simply in the certainty that "I am," one becomes
what Hegel calls a "master," while if one lives simply in the
certainty that "I will die," one becomes what he calls a "slave."
If one says "I will die," according to this, one is saying "I am
subject to death," one is recognizing one's subjection to death.
The slave's consciousness is pervaded, Hegel says, by "the fear
of death, the sovereign master."[22] If one says "I am," on the
other hand, one is not specifically recognizing one's subjection
to death, and if one says "I am" in the face of death, one may

be challenging or even repudiating the sovereignty of death. If one says *Yes*, though, both to "I am" and "I will die," like the man we are imagining, one is recognizing that both the master and the slave dwell within one. Their unity is that of the "I," the self. One is recognizing too that one has been dealing only with the certainties of one's life, however uncertain one may have been about them and however often one may have needed to have them reaffirmed, and not with the real uncertainties.

When one enters, therefore, into the realm of uncertainty, the unknown world of the soul, like the man we are imagining, after having lived mostly in the realm of certainty, the known world of the self, one discovers the possibility of human relationships other than those of master and slave. It is a telling point that Hegel treats of the masters and the slaves under the heading of "self-certainty."[23] What is at stake between masters and slaves is life and death, but life in the form of the certainty that "I am" and death in the form of the certainty that "I will die." When one enters into the realm of uncertainty, what is at stake is life and death in their uncertainty, life and death in the reality that one cannot know until one has lived and died.

To say *Yes* life and death in their uncertainty as well as in their certainty, to say *Yes* to the God who leads one in one's uncertainty as well as grounds one in one's certainty, that seems to be the meaning of Hammarskjöld's "*Yes* to Someone —or Something" and the ultimate answer to his question "Who or what can give me the power to transform the mirror into a doorway?" The man we are imagining says that *Yes* too, it seems, when he sees our life together and chooses it. For what he sees and chooses is an uncertainty as well as a certainty, the uncertainty surrounding the certainty that "I am" and "I will die." That is the paradox of entering the otherworld like Orpheus or Dante while one is still alive. One is entering a realm where one encounters a reality that one will not fully know until one has already lived and died. One encounters that reality now in the form of uncertainty. To see it and choose it, as the man we are imagining is doing, is to trust the God who leads one in one's uncertainty, to trust God's leading and to be willing to be led wherever God will lead.

We spoke earlier in the book (in Chapter 3) of stepping into one's image in the mirror by saying *Yes* to oneself. That was a matter of stepping into the self who says "I am," and it led to a sense of being known by God. Now we are speaking of the mirror that is the entrance and the barrier to the other-world and of stepping into the self who says "I will die." When one does that, one is surrounded by the uncertainty of one's life and death and one may come, like the man we are imagining, to a sense of being led by God in one's uncertainty. We began to see the need of stepping into the self who says "I will die" when we saw the need of letting go of everyone and everything, of going through death in the midst of life (in Chapter 4), and we began to surmise that one who did this would be plunged into the unknown when we saw death under the image of a new and unkown life (in Chapter 5). Now we are seeing the act of stepping into the self who says "I will die" as a move from will to willingness, a *Yes* to the certainty of one's death that leaves one surrounded by the unknown in the form of uncertainty. The sense of uncertainty, knowing that one cannot know what one's life and death will be until one has already lived and died, is the very air of the otherworld for one who is still alive.

What may one hope to find in the realm of the unknown and the uncertain? May one hope to find Eurydice like Orpheus and bring her back with one to the familiar world? May one hope to find Beatrice like Dante and come through her to "the love that moves the sun and the other stars"? To recover one's soul would be to find the missing link between mind and body. It would be to find the unity of one's being. That is the heart's desire, it seems, of one who lives in our historic situation of split between mind and body, between "I am" and "I will die." One is like Nietzsche in the insane asylum, "yearning for two clasped hands to usher in the great miracle—the unity of my being."[24]

7

Recovery of Soul

"I LOST, and then I found, and then I lost again," Ursula says in William Morris' tale, *The Well at the World's End.* "Maybe I shall find the lost once more." Then the Sage answers, "The lost which was verily thine shalt thou find again."[1]

In Morris' tale Ralph meets Ursula in the first quarter of the story, "The Road unto Love," but he gives his love then rather to the Lady of Abundance. Then in the second quarter, "The Road unto Trouble," he loses the Lady of Abundance—she is killed by a disappointed lover. He finds Ursula again in the third quarter, "The Road to the Well at the World's End," and they seek together for the Well. It is then that she speaks of finding and losing and says "Maybe I shall find the lost once more." They do find the Well, and in the last quarter of the story, "The Road Home," they come back together from the World's End and live together happily ever after.

It seems essential to the story that there is not only a man and a woman and their relations with each other but there is also something else, the Well at the World's End. The water of the Well cures sorrow. Yet one can be afraid to drink it. There is an inscription on the Well that reads:

Ye who have come a long way to look upon me, drink of me, if ye deem that ye be strong enough in desire to bear length of days: or else drink not, but tell your friends and the kindreds of the earth how you have seen a great marvel.[2]

All this seems to bear upon our own story. We too have imagined a man and a woman who have found each other and lost one another. There is something else too, like the water of the Well. It is the new and unknown life that each has glimpsed in the other. We have compared it with the "water of night" that Camus speaks of in his story "The Adulterous Woman," and even with the water that Jesus speaks of to the woman at the well in the Gospel of John. The finding and the losing that we have been speaking of is a finding and a losing not only of one another but of this new and unknown life. It is a finding and losing of "soul." If we speak now of finding the lost once again, it is of finding once again the new and unknown life. If the man and the woman we are imagining do find the life, nevertheless, they can also in some way find one another, meet again somehow in the greater life they have found—"The lost which was verily thine shalt thou find again."

If there is a difference between Morris' tale and ours, however, it is between the wisdom of that saying, "The lost which was verily thine shalt thou find again," and the wisdom of this, "He who finds his soul will lose it, and he who loses his soul for my sake will find it." What one finds when one willingly loses the life one has lost may be something greater, something more like the total life of self and soul, the life of "spirit," like the water that Jesus speaks of to the woman at the well, "Whoever drinks of the water that I shall give him will never thirst."[3]

Let us imagine our man and woman setting out once more

to find the new and unknown life, setting out now, though, with the experience that comes from going through loss. Let us allow them to find not just the life of soul but the total life of self and soul, the life of spirit. And let us imagine them meeting one another again in the greater life they come to, meeting where we are most alone.

1. "HE WHO LOSES HIS SOUL FOR MY SAKE WILL FIND IT"

At the beginning of *The Divine Comedy* Dante is "lost in a dark wood."[4] He comes out of the wood, sees a path leading up a hill, and sees the sun rising behind the hill. He begins to take the path but sees ahead of him three beasts lying in wait for him on the way, a leopard and a lion and a wolf. He draws back in dismay and it is then that he meets Vergil who tells him that there is another, darker way, that must be taken, a way that leads down into hell. It is only by taking that dark way, he learns, that he can hope to find Beatrice again, going through hell and purgatory to paradise. He does go down into hell then, Vergil leading him, and on through purgatory, and then in the earthly paradise he does meet Beatrice at last. Then she becomes his guide and leads him from the earthly paradise to the heavenly paradise. There after one last smile she turns from him to the face of God, and he too turns toward God, following her gaze, and never looks back again toward Beatrice.

It seems significant that Dante cannot take the direct path up the hill but must go down through hell and purgatory to paradise. That seems to be in accord with the wisdom of the saying, "He who finds his soul will lose it, and he who loses his soul for my sake will find it." The going through hell seems to be a willing loss of soul that leads through purgatory to finding his soul. If Beatrice is his "soul," as he said in *The Banquet*, and "the life of my heart,"[5] then to find his soul and the life of

his heart is to come into the earthly paradise. It seems significant too, however, that he does not stop with the earthly paradise and the reunion with Beatrice but goes on to the heavenly
paradise and the vision of God, that Dante and Beatrice do not
end facing each other but facing together toward God.

If we are living in a split between mind and body, if loss of
soul is our historic condition, as we have been saying, then we
are in a state like Dante between losing and finding Beatrice. It
may be that the direct path to fulfillment is blocked for us too
and that we too must take the darker way that leads through
hell and purgatory to paradise.

> But why return to such unhappiness?
> Why not be climbing up the lovely hill
> That is the source and reason of all joy?[6]

So Vergil says to Dante when he sees him leaving the direct
path and returning into the dark wood. Then Dante tells him
about the leopard and the lion and the wolf waylaying the path
and Vergil speaks of the other way that leads down through
hell. The direct path is the way the man we have been imagining took when he went on his journey into solitude. He found
God in solitude, "the source and reason of all joy," but he still
felt, even after he had found God, an unfulfilled longing for
intimacy. It was an undifferentiated longing that did not know
whether it longed for God or for a human being. It was dark
and unknowing like the heart of a leopard, fierce and violent
like the heart of a lion, cold and unloving like the heart of a
wolf. He came back to the human circle, hoping his heart
would be transformed into the heart of a human being, and
then he did find his soul and the life of his heart in another
human being, but he lost it again in losing the other, as Dante
did in losing Beatrice. He became "lost in a dark wood," looking for his soul.

He began his descent into hell then, going through the experience of loss, the despair and the desperation, the split between mind and body, and then his passage through purgatory, passing from will to willingness, saying *Yes* to "I will die" as well as to "I am." Now at last the no-man's-land between his mind and his body, after going through a kind of false dawn when he discovered the new and unknown life in another person, is ready for a true dawn.

"False dawn," as it is called, is the faint light that sometimes appears on the eastern horizon before dawn actually begins. It is sunlight reflected by myriads of small particles. It is "false" only in that it is reflected and is not the direct sunlight that begins to appear at dawn. The new and unknown life too, as one first sees it in another person, is a reflection of what it would be if one were to actually live it oneself. The dawn begins when one does begin to live it. The rising sun is like God. The sun rises, according to this, when God appears to be the life not only of the self but also of the soul. That happens, if what we were saying about despair and desperation is true, when one passes from will to willingness. Will as self-will holds the self in the condition that it is already in, the condition of soullessness, and thus defeats its own will to acquire the new life. Willingness as self-surrender allows the self to be changed, to be endowed with soul, to be given the new and unknown life. When one passes from will to willingness, therefore, one's night passes into dawn, one's hell changes into purgatory, the stages of one's journey through hell become stages of a journey through purgatory. One comes to the place where Dante is to meet Beatrice again, where one is to recover one's soul.

It is dawn when Dante enters the earthly paradise where he is to meet Beatrice. It is like dawn on the first day of creation, but because it comes after loss it is even more like dawn on the first day of the week when Jesus rises from the dead. Loss of soul is like death, and recovery of soul is like resurrection. Going through loss of soul, one goes through the letting go of everyone and everything that one is required to go through in death. One has to let go, above all, of the person in whom one has found a new and unknown life, and one has to let go of the life itself. If the loss becomes willing, then one enters into a new relationship with both the person and the life, and that new relationship is somehow a recovery of the person and of the life.

"I lay down my life, that I may take it again,"[7] Jesus says in the Gospel of John. I lay down my life in death, he is saying, that I may take it again in resurrection. Or if we translate *psyche* literally as "soul," as we have been doing, we can turn the formula of death and resurrection into a formula of loss and recovery of soul: "I lay down my soul, that I may take it again." Only by laying down my soul, it seems, by willingly losing the person I have lost, by willingly losing even the new and unknown life I have lost, do I actually recover my soul. Willingly losing the person I have lost is a new relationship with the person, and willingly losing the life I have lost is a new relationship with the life. The new relationship is my willingness itself. Once I stand in the new relationship, the fatality of my old relationship is broken. There was something in the old relationship that led to disaster, that led from finding to losing. There was something in the loss, the unwilling loss, that tended to hold me in a state of soullessness and not allow me to recover. When I willingly let go of the person and the life I have found and lost, I break the spell.

"No one takes it from me, but I lay it down of my own accord," Jesus says of his life. "I have power to lay it down, and I have power to take it again."[8] When I stand in the new relationship of willingness to the person and the life I have lost, when the fatality of my old relationship is broken, then I stand in the "power" that he speaks of here. It seems to be the same power that is spoken of in the prologue to the Gospel of John, "But to all who received him, who believed in his name, he gave power to become children of God."⁹

At every point in our story willingness is enabling and empowering. Willingness to walk alone enables one to enter solitude and find God; willingness to be in need enables one to enter the human circle and find a new and unknown life in another person; and now willingness to let go enables one to recover the life and the person. The "power to become children of God" is the power to stand in the relationship of the Son to the Father. That relationship, we saw earlier (in Chapter 3), is one of knowing and being known, loving and being loved. It is also, we are seeing now, one of laying down one's life or one's soul and taking it again. It is the "power to lay it down" and the "power to take it again," the power of dying and rising. There is an "I and thou" relationship with the Father, but there is also a relationship with the Son. One stands in an "I" that already exists, the "I" of the Son, an "I" that knows and is known, loves and is loved, but also dies and rises, that has already gone through death and resurrection. That is the meaning of "for my sake," it seems, in "He who loses his soul for my sake will find it."

When I say *Yes* to "I am," provided the *Yes* is one of willingness rather than of will, I enter into the place of the Son who knows and is known, loves and is loved. When I say *Yes* to "I will die," again provided the *Yes* is one of willingness rather than of will, I enter into the place of the Son who dies and rises. If the *Yes* is one of will, then something else happens, something like Yeats' "Dialogue of Self and Soul" where soul becomes silent and self has the last word.¹⁰ Then the last word is indeed one of will, one of self-affirmation, and I end simply by willing my own life and death, willing perhaps to live and die again and again like Yeats' "Self" envisioning the prospect of reincarnation, or willing perhaps to live the very same life and die the very same death again and again like Nietzsche's "Superman" (*Übermensch*) envisioning the prospect of "eternal recurrence."[11]

If the *Yes* is one of willingness, then I live neither in the prospect of reincarnation nor in that of eternal recurrence but in that of resurrection. "I am the resurrection and the life,"[12] Jesus says to Martha in the Gospel of John. That is the answer to "I am" and "I will die." When I stand in willingness rather than in will, then self does not have the last word. Soul does not become silent. I recover soul, and in recovering it I recover the missing link between mind and body. I experience a resurrection of the body.

2. GOD, MIND, SOUL, BODY

"We only find what we have lost when we dead awaken," Irene says in Ibsen's last play, *When We Dead Awaken*. "What do we find then?" Rubek asks. "We find that we have never lived,"[13] she answers. That is what we find when we recover soul. If I have been living in our historic condition of split between mind and body and I recover soul, as we are now supposing, my recovery of soul is like an awakening from death. I find that I have never lived, never lived fully as a human being can, never lived as a human being is meant to live. What has been missing? There is a clue in the commandment "You shall love the Lord your God with all your heart, and with all your soul, and with all your might."[14] Living in a split between mind and body, I have never loved anyone or anything with all my heart, and with all my soul, and with all my might.

That is what has happened to the man and the woman in

Ibsen's play. They have "never lived" because they have never loved. He is an aging sculptor and she had been, in youth, the model for his masterpiece, "The Day of Resurrection," posing as a girl awakening from the sleep of death. They had worked together on it for years. "You were my inspiration," he tells her, recalling it all in later life. "I gave you my soul—young and alive," she says, "and left myself empty, soulless."[15] But he had not loved her. It is possible to be inspired by another person, it seems, to be drawn to the new and unknown life one sees in the other, without really loving the other. In fact, it is not possible to love "with all your heart, and with all your soul, and with all your might" until you have found your own soul. Here is a paradox. As long as another person is my "soul" and "the life of my heart," as Beatrice was for Dante when he first met her and, perhaps even more intensely, when he had lost her, I do not yet have the heart and the soul to love the other. It is only when I find my soul by willingly letting go of the other that I become capable of loving with all my heart and all my soul and all my might. And then it is "the Lord your God" that I become capable of loving, though I can be with the other in that love, as Dante was with Beatrice in "the love that moves the sun and the other stars."[16]

It is to such a love that the man and the woman in Ibsen's play seem to aspire when they awaken and realize they have never lived. They climb a mountain together, hoping to reach the sunrise at the peak, and in the original version of the play they reach the peak and the play ends in the sunrise, but in the final version they pass into a storm and perish in an avalanche.[17] Life is over, Ibsen may have believed, when the fullness of life is attained, for it is difficult to imagine human beings sustaining a life of fullness for any length of time. It is particularly difficult for us, living in a historic condition of loss of soul and experiencing the gap that such a condition leaves

between mind and body, to imagine what it would be to recover soul.

Let us try, nevertheless, to envision it. Let us replace the
man and the woman in Ibsen's play with the man and the
woman in the story we have been telling. It is possible, according to our story, to enter into a fullness of life on this side of
death by entering, like the man and the woman we have been
imagining, into the place of the man who died and is risen. It is
possible to come to an awakening in the midst of life like the
one sung in the early Christian hymn:

> Awake, O sleeper,
> And arise from the dead,
> And Christ shall give you light.[18]

Say the man and the woman in our story do awaken. Say
they awaken like the disciples of Jesus did when they became
convinced he was risen from the dead: "I have seen the Lord!",
"We have seen the Lord!" "The Lord is risen indeed!"[19] The
disciples had been with Jesus during his public life; but when
they came to believe he was risen, a hope kindled in their
hearts so great that it was as if they had never lived before, as
if they had been dead themselves and were now awakened
from the dead: "Did not our hearts burn within us while he
talked to us on the road, while he opened to us the scriptures?"[20] It is much the same with the man and the woman in
our story. They have already entered upon the spiritual adventure, like the disciples of Jesus following him during his public
life, but there is something in them that is only now awakening. "When we dead awaken," they can say too, "we find that
we have never lived." What is awakening in them? We have
been calling it "soul" and conceiving it to be the link between
mind and body, between the self that says "I am" and the self
that says "I will die." But what is the link? The hope kindled in

the hearts of the disciples is our clue. "He who believes in me, though he die, yet shall he live," Jesus says to Martha, "and whoever lives and believes in me shall never die."[21]

When such a hope is kindled in our hearts, then something does awaken within us. We dead do awaken. For it is a hope that affects the basic certainties of human existence, "I am" and "I will die." Our hope is ordinarily bounded by these certainties. A human being can hope, we usually suppose, for a life and for well-being in a life within the boundaries of these truths, that he is and that he will die. The words "He who believes in me, though he die, yet shall he live, and whoever lives and believes in me shall never die" invite us to hope for more. If I do actually hope for more, if I do actually hope that "though I die, yet shall I live," then these certainties, "I am" and "I will die," though they remain certain, yet cease for me to be boundaries of hope and of existence. "I am and I will die," I can say, "yet shall I live."

"Despair and die,"[22] the command that is repeated to Richard III by the ghosts of all his victims, reveals how hope and despair are linked with life and death. It is a command to which one is susceptible when one is living in a condition like ours of loss of soul, when there is an open chasm between mind and body, between "I am" and "I will die." It is a demonic command, designed to dissolve completely the unity of a human being when that unity is already impaired. "I am I,"[23] Richard says when he awakens from his nightmare, trying to resist that command, but there is something in him that yields to it. "I shall despair," he says, yielding. "There is no creature loves me; and if I die, no soul will pity me."[24] It is as if the self that says "I am" tries to resist the command to despair and die, but the self that says "I will die" yields to it and obeys. The command is demonic, but that is concealed in Shakespeare's play by the fact that it is addressed to Richard, who is seen there as someone who deserves to die. It is concealed in that same way in actual life. The command to despair and die comes to one in moments when one feels one does not deserve to live.

"Awake, O sleeper, and arise from the dead" is thus a reversal of "Despair and die." It is a command to hope and live. When it comes to one, it takes one beyond the question as to whether one deserves to die or deserves to live. It does not simply encourage the self that says "I am" and quiet the self that says "I will die." Rather, it calls forth a hope that includes "I will die" as well as "I am," a hope that "though I die, yet shall I live," a hope that can go through death without despair. If the command to despair and die is demonic, driving a wedge between mind and body, between "I am" and "I will die," then the command to hope and live is divine, awakening the soul, restoring the circulation of life between mind and body. For when hope does awaken, an entire life awakens along with it. One comes fully to life. It begins to seem indeed that one has never lived before. One awakens to a life that is eternal in prospect, a life that opens up before one all the way to death and beyond, a life that seems able to endure death and survive it.

Whenever hope rises, life rises. When one first enters upon the spiritual adventure, hope rises where there was no hope before, where there was a life of "quiet desperation," and life rises too, the life of the spiritual adventure, the sense of being on a journey in time. There is *something to live for* where before there was nothing. Yet it proves not to be enough. One's heart is kindled, and yet there is a residue of darkness in it that remains unkindled. That dark residue is touched only when one discovers a new and unknown life in another person. When one finds the other, a new hope rises and one seems now to have *someone to live for*, but that hope is disappointed when one loses the other person through death or estrangement. The dark residue in one's heart has been heated but not to the kindling point, the "fire point" after which it will burn by itself. It reaches the kindling point only "when we dead awaken," when one discovers a life that is able to live through death and loss. When the hope of living through death arises, then a life arises within one that appears to be the very life one is hoping for, the life that is spoken of in the words of promise, "and whoever lives and believes in me shall never die."

If mind, as we are conceiving it, is the self that says "I am" and body is the self that says, "I will die," then soul or, more accurately, self endowed with soul is the self that says "yet shall I live." And these three are one. Or, at any rate, the self that is fully awakened, the self endowed with soul, is one and it can say all of these things: "I am and I will die, yet shall I live." A person becomes each of these selves in turn in the course of the spiritual adventure. I become the self that says "I am" when I find something to live for, when I enter upon the spiritual adventure, when I set out upon the journey that will become my story and will answer the question "Who am I?" I become the self that says "I will die" when I find someone to live for, when I discover a new and unknown life in another person, when I realize that I will have to pass through death to enter into the life of the other.

I become the self that says "though I die, yet shall I live," therefore, when I find more than just something or someone, when I find the heart and soul to love, when I find my way through death. Actually this is the self I have been becoming all along, the self endowed with heart and soul. Not only mind but also heart, and heart first of all, comes alive when I enter upon the spiritual adventure; and not only body but also soul, and soul first of all, comes alive when I find a new and unknown life in another person. Still, it is only when I find my way through death that heart and soul come fully to life, that it becomes possible to love "with all your heart, and with all your soul, and with all your might." To love "with all your might" is to love with your whole body, it seems, as when "David danced before the Lord with all his might."[25] It is when heart and soul come fully to life that the link between mind and body is established, that life begins to circulate between mind and body, that one's body becomes caught up in the spiritual adventure.

"Heart and soul," as the phrase is ordinarily used, means "with all one's affections and energies,"[26] and it is probably derived from the phrasing of the commandment to love "with all your heart, and with all your soul, and with all your might." As we have been using the terms, "heart and soul" is more specifically the region between mind and body, "heart" being close to mind and "I am," "soul" being close to body and "I will die." We have also spoken of soul as "a dark residue in the heart" that can remain unkindled when the heart is kindled. Whenever heart and soul come to life, according to our way of speaking, whenever the heart is fully kindled, even the dark residue in the heart, then one becomes capable of acting with all one's affections and energies. It is then that one becomes like a dancer dancing before the Lord with all his might. At those moments the spiritual adventure becomes a dance, and Yeats' question can be asked, "How can we know the dancer from the dance?"[27]

3. "I IN THEM AND THOU IN ME"

There are other moments, though, when the heart is not fully kindled, when the dark residue remains dark. At those moments, when one is not heart and soul in the spiritual adventure, we can know the dancer from the dance. Then it appears that one has entered into a story that is not altogether one's own. One has entered into the story of the man who died and is risen, but one has not yet died and risen oneself. One has gone through a letting-go of everyone and everything like that which takes place in death, but one has not yet gone through actual death. There is a relationship, nevertheless, an "I and thou," that endures even in those darker moments.

"In each *Thou* we address the eternal *Thou*," Martin Buber says in *I and Thou*, and "through contact with every *Thou* we are stirred with a breath of the *Thou*, that is, of eternal life."[28] We come fully to life only in meeting one another, he is saying, and because we do come fully to life in that meeting we appear to have met not only one another but also God. We appear to have met God in one another, to have addressed God, to have been stirred with a breath of God. Yet that breath is not a breath of immortality but a breath of eternal life. We have met a God, he says, "who is not 'immortal' but eternal."[29] When we meet the gods, according to the accounts in the *Iliad* and the *Odyssey*, we are stirred with a breath of immortality. When Odysseus meets the goddess Calypso, for instance, she offers him immortality if he will live with her on her enchanted island. When we meet God, on the other hand, especially when we meet God in one another, it is no longer we mortals with our joy and sorrow meeting immortals with their inextinguishable laughter. Instead, we find a God who, though he does not die, yet knows our sorrow as well as our joy, and we begin to hope that, though we die, yet shall we live.

We are stirred with a breath of immortality when we see a mysterious life in one another and are drawn to one another in the hope of sharing it. That is when we meet the gods in one another. A man meets a goddess and a woman meets a god when, like the man and the woman in our story, they discover a new and unknown life in one another. That mysterious life we see in one another is a breath of immortality, but we always seem to be separated from it by our own mortality. It seems to lie across a gulf of death. "Immortals are mortal, mortals are immortal," Heraclitus says, "they live one another's death and die one another's life."[30]

We are stirred with a breath of eternal life, according to our story, only when we cross that gulf of death, when we pass through loss to reunion, through letting go of one another to being with one another in a new relationship. It is this new relationship, it seems, that is the "I and thou" where we come fully to life in meeting one another, where we meet God in one another and are stirred with a breath of God. When we pass through loss to recovery, however, through death to life, we are entering into the story of the man who died and is risen. We enter, therefore, not simply into an "I and thou" relationship with one another and an "I and thou" with God, but we enter also into a relationship with the man who died and is risen, according to the formula from the Gospel of John, "I in them and thou in me."[31] We enter, that is, into a relationship of indwelling where "I" is that of Jesus dwelling in us and "thou" is that of Abba his God dwelling in him. We enter into an eternal "I and thou," eternal indeed and not immortal, for "I" died and rose, and we are stirred with a breath of eternal life that is the very breath of God, the Spirit.

We enter, nevertheless, into a story that is not altogether our own. That is the problem. What becomes of love and work and communal life in "I in them and thou in me"?

Our story is not altogether our own, we can say, because it is not altogether a story of self. It is a story also of soul. Thus it does not end simply in a return to the familiar. Love between man and woman, for example, when it is seen in terms of self, when it is seen as an episode in a story that is altogether one's own, can appear to be a losing of oneself. Kierkegaard speaks

of "the cleft which threatened to divide my nature" in his love
for Regina. The cleft, as he understands it, is between one and
oneself: the self is losing possession of itself. When one loses
the other person then, as he lost Regina, one regains possession
of oneself. "I am again myself," he says after losing her. "The
cleft which threatened to divide my nature is again closed."[32]

It is actually soul, according to the story we have been telling, that divides one from oneself. Soul comes to life when one
discovers a mysterious life in another person, and it begins
immediately to divide one from oneself as one is drawn out of
one's familiar life, the life of self, and is drawn into the mysterious life one sees in the other, the life of soul. If one loses
the other person then, as Kierkegaard lost Regina or Dante
lost Beatrice, one may try to return to one's familiar life and
be oneself again, but one will still experience the cleft that
threatened to divide one's nature. One will experience it as
a cleft between the self that says "I am" and the self that says
"I will die," a cleft between mind and body, an empty place
where soul ought to be. If one enters then into that empty
place, if one willingly goes through the loss one has suffered,
one comes into a new relationship with the person and the
mysterious life one has lost. One is like Dante finding Beatrice
again in the otherworld. One enters into an "I and thou" relationship with the person one has loved and lost, not an "I"
facing a "thou" as when one was first drawn toward the other,
but an "I and thou" facing together into a life that can be
shared, a life that is not altogether one's own, a life that is
familiar and yet mysterious.

What if the "I and thou" is not mutual? What if the other
person is not aware of the relationship? "Even if the man to
whom I say *Thou* is not aware of it in the midst of his experience," Buber says, "yet relation may exist."[33] Dante's meeting
with Beatrice in the otherworld, as an experience, may have

been no more than a "meeting in a dream,"[34] as it has been called, yet his relationship to Beatrice, as he describes it in that meeting, may have been very real. When a relationship is one-sided, as Dante's was with Beatrice, one may try to realize it, as Dante did in his poetry, by giving expression to it in one's work. All work, according to Hegel, is that: the slave recognizes the master but is not recognized by the master, and so the slave seeks through his work to gain the recognition that he himself gives but does not receive.

"In the master," Hegel says, "the slave feels self-existence to be something external, an objective fact; in fear self-existence is present within himself; in fashioning the thing self-existence comes to be felt explicitly as his own proper being."[35] In the master, that is, the slave comes up against an "I am" that is not his own; in "the fear of death the sovereign master"[36] he is able to say "I" but it is "I will die"; in work he is able to say "I am." Still, it is one thing to say "I am" to oneself and to others through one's work, and it is another thing to say, as Dante does to Beatrice in his work, "I and thou." In Beatrice he comes up against an "I am" that is not his own; in his fear of the death that separates them he is able to say the "I" in "I will die"; and in his work describing his journey across the gulf of death he is able to say "I am." Yet because he really does enter into the relationship with her that he describes, he is able to say "I and thou." Work, therefore, can be more than a process of self-realization; it can say more than "I am." It can realize a relationship; it can say "I and thou."

To enter into an "I and thou" relationship when one has gone through loss is to become heart-free and heart-whole, even if the relationship is not mutual. It is to rise out of our historic condition of conflict between "masters" and "slaves" where some play the role of a self saying "I am" and others play the role of a self saying "I will die." If the "I and thou" relationship *is* mutual, however, as we are supposing in our story, then to enter into it is to meet where we are most alone.

Actually the story we have been telling of quest and loss and recovery is a parable not only of love between man and woman but of other human relationships as well, hope and peace and understanding and friendship. To have hope and peace and understanding and friends is to live the life of the spirit; to be bereft of them is to live in the condition of self without soul. To be sure, there is hope and peace and understanding and even friendship that can exist simply in the relation of self to itself, where we are most alone, but each of these can also be a relation between persons, where we meet, friendship clearly but also understanding each other, peace with each other, hope shared with each other. When they do become relations between persons, we meet where we are most alone, we share the life of the spirit with one another. Thus our story is actually the story of three stages of communal life among human beings. There is first a stage when we are drawn to the mysterious life we see in one another, and it is then that we get our first glimpse of hope and peace and understanding and friendship with one another. Then there can be a stage of loss when we are bereft of these things and reduced to playing the roles of "masters" and "slaves" with each other, to being selves who say "I am" or selves who say "I will die." And then finally there can be a stage when we recover hope and peace and understanding and friendship. It is then, when we come through loss to recovery, that we meet where we are most alone.

Why do we pass through loss? Why is it that in story and in actual experience those who love one another seem always to become separated from one another and have to pass through loss to reunion? Why must we pass through despair and desperation to hope, through conflict to peace, through incomprehension to understanding, and through estrangement to friendship? It is because of the historic emergence of mankind and of the individual, it seems, because the emergence has been also a separation, because mankind has become separated from God and the individual has become separated from mankind. There is a chasm, an historic separation, that can make itself felt in one's personal experience, that has to be crossed in one's personal journey. It can make itself felt between two individuals if they are drawn to one another, and then it has to be crossed if they are to share their lives with one another.

"I in them and thou in me" describes a situation in which the separation no longer holds. It is a formula of indwelling. The individual is no longer separated from mankind, and mankind is no longer separated from God. Yet there is no massive change in human existence. What comes about is simply a relationship, an "I and thou." That simple relationship, though, can bridge the chasm of unrelatedness that exists between the individual and mankind and between mankind and God. There is one who dwells in others, "I in them," and God dwells in him, "and thou in me." The man who died is risen and lives in his followers, and they live in his intimacy with God. They enter, that is, not just into a relationship with the eternal "thou," but they enter into an eternal "I and thou," an eternal intimacy.

Soullessness is unrelatedness. There is a kind of soullessness that comes from living in solitude, like the man in our story, having a relationship with oneself and through oneself to God but having no developed relationship with others. It is the soullessness that comes from the separation of the individual from mankind. There is another kind that comes from living in the human circle, like the woman in our story, having a relationship with others but having no developed relationship with oneself. It is the kind that comes from the separation of mankind from God. There is self in both instances, for there is a life that is familiar and there are relationships that exist in that life. There is a lack of soul, though, for there is a whole realm of relationship that is missing. That missing realm is the mysterious life the man and woman in our story find in one another. They awaken to it when they find it in one another; they awaken to their own lack of it when they lose one another; but they awaken fully when they begin to live it themselves. It is then, when they pass in willingness from finding to losing to living, when they awaken fully to hope, that the man in our story finds "thou," that the woman in our story finds "I," that both of them find "I in them and thou in me.'

Their story is not altogether their own, foɪ they are dealing with a condition that is not altogether their own, an historic condition, a condition that arises out of the history of mankind and the history of the individual. And so they do not simply find themselves and find one another, but they find "I" in the fullest and richest sense, the eternal "I" in the human "I," and they find "thou" in the fullest and richest sense, the eternal "thou" in the human "thou." They enter into an intimacy that is not altogether their own, an eternal intimacy, an eternal "I and thou," and there they find a life that is not altogether their own, an eternal life, a hope, a peace, an understanding, a friendship that can endure death and survive it.

8

The Reasons of the Heart

"IF a man went westward to the end of the world he would find something—say a tree—that was more or less than a tree, a tree possessed by a spirit," Chesterton fancies in *The Man Who Was Thursday*, and "if he went east to the end of the world he would find something else that was not wholly itself —a tower, perhaps, of which the very shape was wicked."[1]

A journey into solitude and back again into the human circle—that is the story we have been telling. It is like a journey to the ends of the earth, westward to the tree and eastward to the tower, the tree being a tree of life, the tower a tower of death. "Alas! I have not yet quite got over expecting the *nouvelle operation* from some human hand," Rilke says in a letter, "and yet why, since my destiny is, as it were, to pass by the human, to reach the uttermost, the edge of the earth."[2] The man in our story has to do that in his journey into solitude, "to pass by the human," to pass by the human circle, that is, "to reach the uttermost, the edge of the earth," to enter into deep solitude. There he finds inexhaustible life. He is like Rilke, though, for he has "not yet quite got over expecting the *nou-*

velle operation from some human hand." He still hopes to find some human being who will change his life, that is, and make him a new man. So he returns to the human circle, and he does indeed find someone. His life is changed and he does become a new man, but he loses the person he has found. His journey back into the human circle becomes, then, a journey to the edge of the earth too, the other edge, a journey through loss and death to life.

"Withdrawal and return,"[3] as Toynbee calls it, is a pattern that can be found throughout human history, especially in the lives of those who have creatively changed the course of human events, like Gotama and Jesus. "Withdrawal" is a journey into solitude, and "return" is a journey back again into the human circle. Gotama, for example, when he was twenty-nine years old, withdrew into the forest, seeking enlightenment, and when he found it he returned again among human beings and spent the remaining years of his life sharing his enlightenment with others. Jesus, too, when he was about thirty years old, withdrew into the desert, and then he returned again for the short duration of his public life to proclaim the kingdom of God. What comes to light in the life of Jesus, though, ending as it does in death and resurrection, is that the return can be more than a simple matter of sharing one's insight with others. It can mean, as in our story, going through loss and death to life.

What happens in the beginning, it may be, decides what shall happen in the end; what happens in the withdrawal decides what shall happen in the return. Our starting point has been the loneliness of the human condition, the loneliness that is not taken away even when one is close to others, the loneliness that appears in the boundary situations of human life: circumstance and conflict and suffering and guilt and death. That loneliness, we have been saying, is an unfulfilled desire

for intimacy, a weak and ineffectual desire, a pining, a languishing. If I enter into solitude, I am confronted with it. How
am I to respond to it?

One way is to seek simply to understand it. If I enter solitude, confront my loneliness, and simply recognize my loneliness for what it is, then I experience an illumining of the
mind. I become enlightened. I realize that my loneliness is that
of the human condition, that it is an unfulfilled desire that lies
at the heart of human life, at the heart of our unhappiness in
circumstance and conflict and suffering and guilt and death. I
come to understand why it is that "the mass of men lead lives
of quiet desperation."[4] My understanding does not take away
desire. It is still there, weak and ineffectual, a pining, a languishing. My heart is not released. My enlightenment, therefore, cannot match that of Gotama, the fully enlightened man,
the Buddha, who was able to say, "Sure is my heart's release."[5] Yet the desire, once I understand it, can no longer
play the role it formerly played in my life. It can no longer
overshadow my life. Instead of unhappy desire I have a new
source out of which to live, namely understanding.

If I am unwilling to stop at understanding, though, if I
choose to follow my heart's desire, however unhappy, if I live
in the hope of fulfillment, then I enter upon a spiritual adventure like that in our story. I experience a kindling of the heart.
My heart's desire waxes instead of waning. It ceases to be weak
and ineffectual. It becomes a powerful longing, an absorbing
passion. The loneliness becomes a love that appears to be
"from God and of God and towards God." I enter upon a road
like that of Jesus, for heart's desire carries me toward God and
toward other human beings, but it also makes me vulnerable to
loss and to suffering. To be happy on the road of heart's desire,
I find, is not so much to experience "the cessation of pain"
when the mind is illumined but "to feel in oneself an excess of

strength" when the heart is kindled and "to know for certain that you are fulfilling the will of God"[6] when you are following the path of heart.

There is an illumining of the mind, nevertheless, that comes from following the heart's desire. It arises out of the kindling of the heart. In fact, the mind is illumined again and again, as the heart is kindled again and again, along the road of the spiritual adventure. At every turn in the road a new illumining is needed to find the way and a new kindling is needed to follow the way. The kindling comes first and leads to the illumining. Before the kindling takes place the mind sees only "how things stand." After it takes place the mind can see how "all things are possible." I may feel, for instance, at a given point in my life's journey that I am condemned to solitude. It may seem to me that I am incapable of loving another human being. Or it may be that I am so afraid of my own heart that, though I love, I don't dare come out of my solitude. It may seem to me that my journey in life is meant to be solitary and so I can never share my life with another human being. That, it may seem, is "how things stand" with me. It may even seem to be "how things stand" with all mankind. It may seem that everyone is condemned to solitude, that no one is capable of love, that no one dares emerge from solitude, that everyone is on a solitary journey.

When my heart's desire is kindled, however, then everything seems otherwise to my mind. Things that seemed impossible begin to seem possible. It begins to seem indeed that "all things are possible." As long as my heart's desire was weak, it seemed impossible to escape from solitude. When it becomes strong, not only does it begin to seem possible to escape, but solitude no longer seems to be a prison. A happy aloneness begins to seem possible. As long as my heart's desire was ineffectual, I seemed incapable of love. When it becomes powerful, not only do I begin to seem capable of love but I seem to be already caught up in a love that comes from God, passes into human beings, and goes to God. As long as my heart's desire was weak and ineffectual, it was also timid and I did not trust it or dare enter into a relationship with God or with another human being. When it becomes strong and powerful, it also becomes daring and I become able to trust it and act upon it. As long as my heart's desire was only a pining and a languishing, it seemed to be no essential part of my life, only a kind of dissatisfaction that tended to undermine my life, which seemed meant therefore to be essentially a solitary journey. When it becomes a powerful longing and an absorbing passion, heart's desire begins to seem essential to my life and makes my life seem meant to be a journey with God and with other human beings.

When my mind has been illumined like this again and again, as my heart has been kindled again and again, I begin to see how I am led along the path of the spiritual adventure, how God leads by kindling the heart and illumining the mind. I begin to see the kindling and the illumining as an experience of being touched by God, and I begin to see God as one who touches hearts and minds and by touching them dissolves the necessity of the human condition into possibility. I begin to see how "God is spirit."

"Is there a God?" yields as a question to "What is God?" when I enter upon the spiritual adventure. For to enter upon the journey is to enter into a relationship with God. It is to enter into an intimacy, a to-and-fro with God. As long as my heart is not kindled, the thought of an intimacy with God, of being known by God, even of being loved by God, can be terrifying. There is a longing for intimacy in the loneliness that pervades the human condition, but there is also a fear. It is the fear, it seems, that renders the longing weak and ineffectual, that reduces it to a pining and a languishing. As long as fear is strong and longing is weak, as long as there is no developed relationship with God, then there is a question about the existence of God. When the spiritual adventure begins, though, when longing becomes so powerful that it "casts out fear," when there is a relationship with God, then there is no more question about the existence of God. "What is God?" is the question, and an answer arises out of the spiritual adventure: "God is spirit."

An illumining and a kindling is a knowing and a loving. It is also an experience of being known and being loved. Thus it is a to-and-fro with God. The "to" is in knowing and loving, the "fro" in being known and being loved. The to-and-fro is the movement of the Spirit, as in the saying "The wind blows where it wills, and you hear the sound of it, but you do not know whence it comes or whither it goes." Say I am at an impasse in my life. I wait for "how things stand" to give way to "all things are possible." I am caught between fear and longing and I wait for my heart to be kindled. Then the kindling comes and the illumining, and I see my way out of the impasse. What I experience is the kindling and the illumining itself—"you hear the sound of it." What eludes me is God the unknown—"you do not know whence it comes or whither it goes." When I say "God is spirit," therefore, I seem to know what God is, but all I actually know is the kindling and the illumining that come from God and carry one toward God. I know God in and through a relationship. I know the to-and-fro with God, the movement of the Spirit. I know what it is to be led along the road of the spiritual adventure.

"What is God?" yields then as a question to "Who is God?" What I know of God is from a relationship, an "I and thou" with God, and that is more apt to tell me *who* God is than *what* God is. If I am willing to be led by God, to live in a to-and-fro with God, to know and be known, love and be loved, then I find myself inside the intimacy described in the saying "No one knows the Son except the Father, and no one knows the Father except the Son." God is called "Master of the Universe" (*Ribbono shel Olam*)⁷ in Jewish prayer. To be intimate with God, then, is to be intimate with the Master of the Universe; to walk with God is to walk with the Master of the Universe. The thought of it is overwhelming.

If I do walk with God, I may be led out of solitude and into the human circle. For with all the kindling and illumining that come about in solitude there is something in me that remains unkindled and unillumined. Who God is remains partly undisclosed. I have followed my heart's desire into solitude, thinking it was a desire for God, but my heart doesn't seem to know whether it longs for God or for a human being. When I find God in solitude and come to walk with God, my heart doesn't know whether it has found its fulfillment or whether it has still to search. My life becomes a journey in time and God becomes my companion on the way, but I am left with an unfulfilled yearning for human companionship. I walk with God, but I find myself longing for a companion who is visible and tangible. At times it can seem that God is not enough for me. Yet at other times, when I think of walking with the Master of the Universe, the thought of intimacy with God is so overwhelming that God seems enough and more than enough. If I am still unfulfilled, I guess then, it is because I have further to walk with God than I have walked.

What is lacking? I enter into a relationship with God in solitude, but I do not bring my entire life with me into the relationship. I bring the part of my life that belongs to solitude, my relationship with myself, but not the part that belongs to the human circle, my relationship with others. By relating to myself and willing to be myself, as Kierkegaard says, I am "grounded transparently"⁸ in God. Yet there is a part of me that remains unrelated and unwilled and ungrounded, and that is the part of me that belongs to the human circle. I relate to myself in solitude when I become aware of the deep loneliness that pervades my life and is not taken away when I am with others. I become willing to be myself when I become willing to follow the longing in my loneliness as my heart's desire. I become grounded transparently in God when I see how I am being led by the illumining of my mind and the kindling of my heart. I am relating to myself but not yet to others; I am willing to walk alone but not yet to be in need of others; and so I find God in solitude but not yet in the human circle. I am relating to God through myself but not yet through others, and so I feel the lack not as a lack of God so much as a lack of human companionship.

To find God in the human circle, to come to relate to God through others, can be a long journey. For the individual seems to have become separated from mankind in history, and mankind seems to have become separated from God in prehistory. I find myself at a second remove, therefore, from a situation in which human beings are at one with one another and with God. Still, the loneliness that has come to light and become acute with the emergence of the individual is a loneliness that lies at the heart of the human condition. All human hearts dwell in the same loneliness. If I follow the longing in that loneliness, the longing for relatedness, I can hope that it will take me not only to God but also to the heart of mankind.

It is at this point that I begin to look for someone who will change my life and make me a new man. Or, if I do not actively look for someone, I become ready at any rate to find someone. I have already found *something* that has changed my life and made me a new man, namely the spiritual adventure. I have found something to live for, the journey with God. Yet my yearning for human companionship on the journey has led me to believe that the change is still incomplete, that the new man has not fully emerged. So now I hope to find *someone*. In finding something to live for I have come to a sense of *what* God is; in entering upon the spiritual adventure I have come to see how "God is spirit." Now in finding someone to share the journey with I hope I will come to a sense of *who* God is; in meeting someone who will change my life and make me a new man I hope I will come into the fullness of an "I and thou" with God.

At this point, it is true, "I have not yet quite got over expecting the *nouvelle operation* from some human hand," as Rilke says, hoping to find someone who will change my life, that is, and make me a new man. I have not yet seen it as an expectation I need to "get over." I have not yet realized how wide a gulf separates mankind from God and the individual from mankind. Still and all, my hopes are not entirely vain. Say I do find someone. I am drawn to a mysterious life, "an unknown life," as Proust calls it, that I see in another person. "A new life begins," I can say like Dante when he has met Beatrice. Until now the spiritual adventure has been for me a journey in solitude. Now it becomes a journey in the human circle. That is the "new life" for me, the spiritual adventure carried into the human circle and brought to its fullness. The unknown and mysterious life I see in the other person is the life of the human circle, a life that is familiar to the other but unfamiliar to me, just as the life of solitude is familiar to me and unfamiliar, let us say, to the other. We are drawn to one another, hoping to share in one another's life.

We have each found *someone*, we have found one another, but we have each found *something* as well, we have found a new and unknown life. In fact, it is *what* we have found in one another not *whom* we have found that makes the difference. We have not yet learned to love one another. What we love is the new and unknown life we have discovered in one another. Thus who God is still remains dark to us. What has come to light is the familiar and the unfamiliar life, "self" and "soul," who we are and who we are not, and how both belong to what we are as human beings.

But what if we lose one another? What if we are separated from one another by death like Dante and Beatrice or by estrangement like Kierkegaard and Regina? Then it becomes clear that we do not yet actually live the new and unknown life we have found in one another. When the other person is gone, I am bereaved of the person and bereft of the new life. I am left with a sense of loss. According to a traditional image of hell, there is a twofold pain in hell. There is the "pain of sense" that arises from the everlasting fire, and there is the "pain of loss"[9] that arises from the everlasting loss of God. When I lose a person in whom I have found a new and unknown life, I suffer a pain that seems very like the "pain of loss."

I have not lost God, it is true, but I have lost a person through whom I was beginning to find a new relationship with God. I have lost "soul." I have come to experience in myself the gap between mankind and God and between the individual and mankind. The gap was already there in me. It was a gap between mind and body, between "I am" and "I will die." These are the basic certainties of human existence, "I am" and "I will die," and yet they have a history. There is a story implicit in "I am," the story of the emergence of the individual, of the separation of the individual from mankind; and there is a story implicit also in "I will die," the story of the emergence of mankind, of the separation of mankind from God. There has been a continuation of the story in the centuries from the Black Death until our own time. The opposition between "I am" and "I will die" has become sharper. The basic loneliness of the human condition has become more acute. Solitary individuals have appeared, like Kierkegaard and Nietzsche and Dostoevsky and Kafka, who live in the most extreme loneliness. When I find a new life in another person, I begin to reverse the whole history of separation. When I lose the person in whom I have found new life, though, I am plunged into the extreme loneliness that is the final fruit of that history.

How are we to pass through the extreme loneliness of our times and come into a relatedness with one another and with God? That extreme loneliness is what I left behind me when I entered upon the spiritual adventure. Now I am plunged back into it by losing the person upon whom I set my heart. I already have a way of coming out of it by following the longing in it as my heart's desire. Now that I have met with loss, however, I have come to an impasse unless I am willing to go through the loss. I cannot follow my heart's desire as long as my heart is set upon the person I have lost, for my heart will only lead me back again and again into the impasse of desiring someone I cannot have. It will lead me again and again to the point where I have to say to myself "There is no hope."

I can follow my heart only if I become heart-free and heart-whole. That means going through a letting-go of everyone and everything such as one is called upon to go through on one's deathbed. It means letting go of the person in whom I have found new life and letting go even of the new life I have found. If I do let go, I become heart-free and heart-whole. I go through a kind of purgatory in which my heart is purified. I pass through death to life. The death I go through is like real death on the deathbed, for I have to let go of everyone and everything, above all to let go of the person on whom my heart is set and of the new and unknown life I had hoped to attain through that person. Yet in letting go I do not abandon hope. It is not the same as saying to myself "There is no hope." Rather, I let go in the hope of recovery. I am like a sick man on his deathbed who is willing to die and yet hopes to live. I am willing to let go of the person and the life I have found and yet I hope to recover the person and live the life. Instead of giving up in despair or fighting on in desperation, I am letting go in hope.

If I set my heart upon another person, then I cannot live without that person. My heart becomes divided. If I give my heart to my life, on the other hand, if I give my heart to the journey with God, then my heart becomes whole and I can be whole in a relationship with another. I can be heart and soul in the relationship because I am heart and soul in the journey of my life. When I let go of another person in hope, I become able to give my heart to my life without cutting off all relationship with the other. Or, vice versa, when I give my heart to my life, to the journey with God, I become capable of letting go of the other person in hope. Say I do give my heart to the spiritual adventure, to the journey with God, and say I do let go of the person in whom I have found new life, say I let go in hope. What happens is that I enter into a new relationship with the person I have found and lost. I enter into a relationship in which my heart is whole and no longer divided. The new relationship is a recovery of the person I have lost. It is a realization of the new life I have found. As I pass from the old relationship to the new, from a divided to a whole heart, my hope begins to be fulfilled. And as I enter upon fulfillment my hope grows ever stronger. I begin to hope that "all shall be well and all manner of thing shall be well."[10]

I end up giving my heart entirely to the journey with God. It is the choice I have been making all along in the spiritual adventure. I give my heart to the journey with God in solitude, according to our story, and then also to the journey with God in the human circle. I relate to God through my relationship with myself, that is, and then also through my relationship with

others. I enter into a kind of paradise where we walk with
God, like Adam and Eve who "heard the sound of the Lord
God walking in the garden in the cool of the day,"[11] but I
bring into paradise the bittersweet taste of the loneliness from
which I have come.

"It is not joy and sorrow which are opposed to one another,
but the varieties within the one and the other," Simone Weil
says. "There are an infernal joy and pain, a healing joy and
pain, a celestial joy and pain."[12] That describes very well the
divine comedy I have to go through to enter the paradise of
walking with God. The striking thing about it is that there is
joy even in hell and pain even in heaven. There is an infernal
pain of loss in losing a person in whom I have found new life,
and there is also an infernal joy of relief at not having to
surrender myself or give up the life with which I am familiar.
There is a healing joy in the hope of recovering the person and
the new life, and there is a healing pain in letting myself feel
the loss and in willingly going through the loss. There is a
celestial joy in actually recovering all I have lost, and there is a
celestial pain in surrendering myself and giving up my familiar
life to live the greater life of the journey with God.

"Who is God?" is answered implicitly in the "I and thou" of
the journey with God. There are two poles of the journey,
according to our story, one in solitude and the other in the
human circle. They are like the tree and the tower at the two
ends of the earth. At one pole, the one in solitude, the questions are "Who am I?" and "What is God?" When I enter upon
the spiritual adventure, I enter into a new story and I come
therefore to a new answer to the question "Who am I?" The
question about God in solitude, though, is "What is God?" For
I have the experience in solitude of drawing upon an inexhaustible source of life. The more I rely upon it the more it
sustains me, and yet it leaves desire unsatisfied. Following my

unsatisfied heart's desire, I am led to the other pole, the one in the human circle. There the questions are rather "What am I?" and "Who is God?" When I follow my heart's desire, I become aware of my human needs, how we live each other's death and die each other's life. I come to an answer, therefore, to the question "What am I?" The question about God in the human circle, though, is "Who is God?" For I have the experience of being heart-free and heart-whole in the human circle only in relationship with God, only in an "I and thou" with God.

It is an eternal "I and thou." Or so it appears in a vision of God that is explicitly Christian, where I see myself entering into the relationship of Jesus with the God he called "Abba" and passing with Jesus through death to life. I enter into the intimacy of Jesus and Abba when I come to terms with the first basic certainty of human existence, "I am," when I let it stand within the eternal "I and thou." I pass with Jesus through death to life when I come to terms with the other basic certainty, "I will die," when I let it stand too within the eternal "I and thou."

There is an uncertainty surrounding these certainties, "I am" and "I will die," and it is out of the uncertainty that the questions arise, "Who am I?" and "What is God?" and "What am I?" and "Who is God?" If I live simply in my certainty about my life and death, then I live simply at the point where we are in the story of mankind, where mankind has become separated from God and the individual has become separated from mankind; I live as a solitary individual. If I live in my uncertainty, on the other hand, I enter upon an adventure like the one we have been describing, a journey into solitude and back again into the human circle. The journey into solitude is a plunge into the uncertainty surrounding "I am," and the journey back again into the human circle is a plunge into the uncertainty surrounding "I will die." If I do enter upon the spiritual adventure, I cease to live as a solitary individual. I come to live in the eternal "I and thou" where mankind is no longer separated from God and the individual is no longer separated from mankind. I go through a reversal of the story of mankind, beginning where it ends, in the deep loneliness of the solitary individual, and ending where it begins, with human beings walking and speaking with God.

What comes to light in the spiritual adventure is the heart's desire. It proves to be a desire for relatedness. It can be felt very sharply in a condition like ours of unrelatedness where the individual is separated from mankind and mankind is separated from God. If I follow my heart's desire, it will lead me into solitude, into a relatedness with myself, and it will lead me into the human circle, into a relatedness with others, but it will lead me ultimately, both in solitude and in the human circle, into a relatedness with God. As I come to know my own heart, I come to know the hearts of others and even the heart of God. "Here is what faith is," Pascal says, "God sensible to the heart, not to reason."[13] Yet when the heart is kindled, the mind is illumined, we have found, and so when God becomes sensible to the heart, he becomes luminous to the mind.

Insight occurs, we can say, when the heart's reasons become known to the mind. That is how insight seems to occur in the great religions of the world, as when Buddha says "Sure is my heart's release" or when Confucius speaks of "looking straight into one's heart and acting on the results"[14] or when Laotzu speaks of man at his best "living clear down in his heart."[15] There are common insights that occur in the emergence of mankind and in the emergence of the individual. There is a consciousness of human mortality that appears in the *Epic of Gilgamesh* and in much traditional human wisdom, the insight in "I will die"; and there is a consciousness of the loneliness of the human condition that appears among the solitary individuals of our times, the insight in "I am." Both insights are enhanced in the experience we have been describing of withdrawal and return. When we withdraw into solitude, "I am" can fade before "It is" as in the formula of the Upanishads, "You are that,"[16] but it can also be caught up in the great "I am" that is uttered by God in Exodus and by Jesus in the Gospel of John. And when we return to the human circle, "I will die" can be caught up in "I am the resurrection and the life." "If anyone worships Muhammad, Muhammad is dead," Abu Bakr said at Muhammad's death, "if anyone worships God, God is living and undying."[17] But Jesus is alive. If we walk in his intimacy with God, if we follow him through loss and death, he is alive in us, we are alive in an eternal "I and thou."

A Note on Method

I N his *Discourse on Method* Descartes bases his method on a single certainty, "I am." If I were to compare and contrast the method I have been using with that of Descartes, I would have to say that method for me is based rather on a twofold certainty, "I am" and "I will die."

It is that other certainty, "I will die," that plays the chief role in my first book, *The City of the Gods*. It actually decided the subject matter of the book. I had originally set out to write a book on the political theology of the Greek city-states. It was to be part of a larger work tracing political theology from ancient times to the present. As I compiled material for it, though, I had the feeling I was piling up lumber. My heart was elsewhere, and it was drawing my mind along after it. I was becoming very concerned at that time about the fact that I must someday die. I was thirty years old and was becoming very conscious that my youth was passing. That was upon my heart, and it came to be upon my mind as well. I became very excited reading the *Epic of Gilgamesh*. It is the story of a man whose best friend died and who went then in search of unending life, who traveled to the ends of the earth but found wisdom rather than life. I saw myself in a position very like that of Gilgamesh, and I began to see a quest like his running through all history. So I changed the subject of my book. I began to write on man's quest of life through the ages. I came in the end to formulate the question "If I must die someday, what can I do to fulfill my desire to live?" It seemed to me, as I completed the book, that all answers to that question had failed, as with Gilgamesh, except one: "He who believes in me, though he die, yet shall he live, and whoever lives and believes in me shall never die."

Every age of history has its answer to the question of death, I found, and the failure of one age and one answer leads to the rise of a new age and a new answer. Since the question for me had arisen out of my own life, though, I wondered if individuals have their own answers to death. An individual has his "life and times." There is a prevailing answer to death in his times. Is there also, I now asked, an answer in his life?

There is, I began to see, in that "I am" is an answer to "I will die." It is "I am," accordingly, that plays the chief role in my second book, *A Search for God in Time and Memory*. When I became sharply conscious of mortality, my life opened up before me all the way to death. At first my attention was focused on death and I was seeing everything from the standpoint of "I will die," but then my attention shifted to the life that had opened up before me and I began to see things from the standpoint of "I am." My second book was to be about lives, I decided, as my first book was about times. I started by telling my own story, sketching out my autobiography, not for inclusion in the book but to prepare myself to understand the stories of others. Then I went on to examine the stories of others, especially in our own age. "I am" is the standpoint of autobiography throughout the ages, starting with the *Confes-*

sions of Augustine. It is also an historic answer to death, I found, the answer of our own age—thus its importance in the method of Descartes. Yet it lacks something as an answer to death. "I am" and "I will die" are certainties, but the important thing, it seemed to me, is hidden in the uncertainty of life and death. To find God, I came to believe, we must give over the quest of certainty for a quest of understanding.

How are we to come to understanding? By passing over to the standpoint of other lives and times and coming back to that of our own lives and times. By passing over, as I realized I had been doing, to Gilgamesh saying "I will die" and coming back to myself saying "I will die." By passing over to Augustine or Descartes saying "I am" and coming back to myself saying "I am."

It is "passing over" and "coming back," therefore, that play the chief role in my third book, *The Way of All the Earth*. When my life opened up before me all the way to death, I became very lonely. "I will die" had raised a question for me, that of life in the prospect of death, but "I am" had raised a question too, though it is an historic answer to death, that of the loneliness of the individual. It is a loneliness that I had seen emerge very strongly in autobiography in the nineteenth and twentieth centuries. I tended to look to a companionship with God rather than to a human companionship to answer it, for it is a loneliness in the face of death, a loneliness that is not taken away even when we are close to one another. Still, I felt a longing also for human companionship. "My life is a journey in time," I wrote in a diary, "and God is my companion on the way. Sometimes I wish it were more literally a journey, and that I had a human companion, visible and tangible." I decided to explore the possibilities of companionship with God. I had passed over to times in my first book, to lives in my second, and now in my third, I decided, I would pass over to

religions, to see how God comes among us and how we walk
with God.

There is an experience that is common to the great religions,
I came to believe, an experience of human wholeness, as in the
formula, "with all your heart, and with all your soul, and with
all your might," but there is a difference of insight into the
experience, a difference between the enlightenment of
Gotama, for example, and the revelation of Jesus. Gotama
walked alone, but Jesus walked in an intimacy with God. I
found it fascinating that someone could walk alone and yet be
whole, but I continued to seek wholeness myself in walking
with God.

"Passing over" would be an answer to loneliness, going over
into the standpoint of another, if it were not for "coming
back," returning to the standpoint of self. It is that standpoint
of return, of self saying "I am" and "I will die," that plays the
chief role in my fourth book, *Time and Myth*. It was there on
home ground, I believed, that I had to find wholeness. In passing over I had found myself entering into stories, epic stories
like that of Gilgamesh, life stories like that of Augustine, stories of enlightenment and revelation like those of Gotama and
Jesus. In coming back I had to ask the question, "What kind of
story am I in?" or, since I had always thought of my readers
and my listeners as passing over with me, "What kind of story
are we in?" It is the story of a spiritual adventure, I began to
see, not just a story of the things of life, how everything that
belongs to a life shall enter into it and how all things must pass,
but a story of relating to the things of life, of relating to their
entering and to their passing, of living a deeper life while
things enter and pass, a life that can endure death and survive
it.

I began actually to tell the story of the spiritual adventure.
At first I told it by retelling the stories into which I had been

passing over, letting the persons in them become one person and letting the stories themselves become one story; but then I began to experiment, as I had done already in a parable in my third book, with simply telling the story myself.

It is the spiritual adventure, the changing standpoint of a person who says "I am and I will die, yet shall I live," that plays the chief role in this my fifth book, *The Reasons of the Heart*. My sense of the spiritual adventure as I began to write was that of a journey with God. Yet I felt an unresolved loneliness. What happened during the three years I spent writing the book is that I went through the loneliness to a sense of being heart-free and heart-whole in the journey with God. I envisioned a person going out to meet his loneliness in solitude and then returning to meet it again in the human circle. It is a loneliness that belongs to our times, that goes with "I am" and the emergence of the individual; but it is also a loneliness that belongs to the human condition, that goes with "I will die" and the emergence of mankind. I had the person I was imagining go into solitude and let "I am" be caught up in the "I and thou" of the journey with God; and then I had him return to the human circle and let "I will die" be caught up in the "I and thou." I ended where I had begun, therefore, in a journey with God, but everything had changed, "I am" and "I will die" and also "I and thou."

There is an historic split, I found, between self saying "I am" and self saying "I will die," a split, that is, between mind and body. It is healed, I came to believe, when one recovers soul, the missing link between mind and body, and that comes about when one is heart and soul in the journey with God.

My method is my journey. It began as a journey like that of Gilgamesh, searching through time, going from one figure to another, looking for an answer to death. Then it became a journey like that of Augustine, searching through memory, my own memory and the memory of others. Then it became a kind of odyssey, passing over into the great religions and coming home again to Christianity and to my own life. Then it became a spiritual adventure paralleling the adventures I entered upon in other lives and times. And now it has become a journey into solitude and back again into the human circle. It has become more and more a journey with God, and the way of being led upon it has become more and more apparent. There is always a kindling of the heart and an illumining of the mind. Each step of the journey begins as a kindling of the heart and ends as an illumining of the mind. Here is the essence of my journey. It is an adventure of the heart that is always becoming also an adventure of the mind.

Notes

PREFACE

1. From Robert Frost's poem "The Road Not Taken" in *Complete Poems of Robert Frost* (New York: Holt, 1949), p. 131.
2. Søren Kierkegaard, *The Concept of Dread*, trans. Walter Lowrie (Princeton, N.J.: Princeton University Press, 1957), p. 143.
3. See Chapter 2, note 16.
4. Matthew 10:39. See also Chapter 6, note 4.
5. See Chapter 5, note 25.
6. See Chapter 6, note 7.
7. Martin Lings, *A Sufi Saint of the Twentieth Century* (Berkeley and Los Angeles: University of California Press, 1971), p. 28.
8. On the way of "no self" (*anatta*) see my book, *The Way of All the Earth* (New York: Macmillan, 1972), pp. 56, 154, and 180.
9. Pascal, *Pensées*, 474 (my translation). I used the edition by Jacques Chevalier in Pascal, *Oeuvres Completes* (Paris: Gallimard, Bibliothèque de la Pleiade, 1954), p. 1221.

CHAPTER 1

1. T. E. Lawrence, *Seven Pillars of Wisdom* (Harmondsworth, England: Penguin and Jonathan Cape, 1971), p. 364.
2. *Ibid.*, p. 366.
3. Willard Ropes Trask, *The Unwritten Song*, vol. 1 (New York: Macmillan, 1966), p. 80.
4. Lawrence, *loc. cit.*
5. Isak Dinesen (Karen Blixen), *Last Tales* (New York: Random House, 1957), pp. 338f.
6. "In order to live happily I must be in agreement with the world. And that is what 'being happy' *means*. I am then, so to speak, in agreement with the alien will on which I appear dependent. That is to say: 'I am doing the will of God.'" Ludwig Wittgenstein, *Notebooks, 1914–1916*, trans. G. E. M. Anscombe (New York: Harper, 1969), p. 75.
7. Franz Kafka, *Tagebücher* (New York: Schocken, 1949), p. 475 under May 4, 1915. (My translation.)
8. Rainer Maria Rilke, *The Notebooks of Malte Laurids Brigge*, trans. M. D. Herter Norton (New York: Norton, 1964), p. 209.
9. "I know whence I have come and whither I am going" (John 8:14);

"Jesus knowing that the Father had given all things into his hands, and that he had come from God, and was going to God" (13:3); "I came from the Father, and have come into the world; again, I am leaving the world, and going to the Father" (16:28). Here and throughout, unless otherwise noted, I am using the Revised Standard Version (1952 and 1972).

10. "I am the bread of life" (John 6:35; cf. 6:51); "I am the light of the world" (8:12); "I am the door" (10:9); "I am the good shepherd" (10:11, 14); "I am the resurrection and the life" (11:25); "I am the way, the truth, and the life" (14:6); "I am the true vine" (15:1, 5).

11. John 17:23.

12. See the article on Al-Hallaj by Louis Massignon and Louis Gardet in *The Encyclopedia of Islam*, vol. 3 (Leiden, the Netherlands: E. J. Brill; and London: Luzac, 1971), p. 100B. See also Herbert Mason, "The Death of Al-Hallaj: A Dramatic Narrative" in *American Poetry Review* (July-August 1974), p. 33 ("The Truth has entered me, I am the Truth, no longer I myself").

13. Mason, *op. cit.*, p. 37.

14. *The Gospel of Sri Ramakrishna* (originally recorded in Bengali by M., a disciple of Ramakrishna), trans. Swami Nikhilananda (New York: Ramakrishna-Vivekananda Center, 1973), p. 726. (I have substituted "ardor" for "prema.")

15. Dinesen, *op. cit.*, p. 26.

16. John 16:28.

17. John 16:29.

18. John 4:14.

19. Otto Rank, *Beyond Psychology* (New York: Dover, 1958), p. 196.

20. John 4:32 and 34.

21. John 6:35.

22. *Antony and Cleopatra*, Act I, scene 3, line 42.

23. See John 5:24 and I John 3:14.

CHAPTER 2

1. *Evangelium Veritatis* (Jung Codex), ed. Michel Malinine, Henri-Charles Puech, Gilles Quispel (Zurich: Rascher, 1956), p. 94 (lines 13ff.).

2. Albert Camus, *The Myth of Sisyphus*, trans. Justin O'Brien (New York: Vintage, 1955), p. 49.

3. Saint Thomas Aquinas, *Summa Theologiae*, I, q. 2, introduction (my translation). I am using here and throughout the Marietti edition (Rome and Turin, 1950).

4. The way of negation is described in Aquinas, *op. cit.*, I, q. 3, introduction (the phrase there is "quomodo Deus non sit"). It runs from q. 3 through q. 13. The way of affirmation is introduced by the last article (a. 12) of q. 13, "Whether affirmative propositions can be formed of God," and runs, I would say, through the rest of the *Summa Theologiae*.

On the way of negation see also the *Summa Contra Gentiles* (Rome: Leonine Manual Edition, 1934), I, 14, where it is called the "via remotionis."

5. Wittgenstein, *op. cit.*, p. 79 ("Wie sich alles verhält, ist Gott. Gott ist, wie sich alles verhält"). Cf. the passage cited above, Chapter 1, note 6, on agreement with the world as equivalent to agreement with the will of God.

6. "Situations like the following: that I am always in situations; that I cannot live without struggling and suffering; that I cannot avoid guilt; that I must die—these are what I call boundary situations," writes Karl Jaspers, *Philosophy*, trans. E. B. Ashton, vol. 2 (Chicago and London: University of Chicago Press, 1970), p. 178. On the idea that "we are alone and we cannot make one another unalone," see my book *Time and Myth* (Garden City, N.Y.: Doubleday, 1973), pp. 103ff.

7. Aquinas, *Summa Theologiae*, I, q. 12, a. 1 and I-II, q. 3, a. 8.

8. *Ibid.*, q. 3, introduction.

9. Immanuel Kant, *Critique of Pure Reason*, trans. F. Max Müller (Garden City, N.Y.: Doubleday, 1966), pp. 222f.

0. *Evangelium Veritatis*, p. 89 (lines 9ff.), p. 90 (lines 9ff.), and p. 96 (lines 32f.).

11. Kafka, "Reflections on Sin, Pain, Hope, and the True Way," #24, in *The Great Wall of China*, trans. Willa and Edwin Muir (New York: Schocken, 1970), p. 167.

12. Kafka, "He," *ibid.*, p. 159 ("The strength to deny, that most natural expression of the perpetually changing, renewing, dying reviving human fighting organism, we possess always, but not the courage, although life is denial, and therefore denial affirmation").

13. Exodus 33:20 (King James Version with modified word order).

14. Baruch Spinoza, *Ethics*, V, 36, trans. R. H. M. Elwes in *The Chief Works of Benedict de Spinoza*, vol. 2 (New York: Dover, 1951), p. 264.

15. Søren Kierkegaard, *The Sickness unto Death* (published with *Fear and Trembling*), trans. Walter Lowrie (Garden City, N.Y.: Doubleday, 1954), pp. 173f.

16. Dag Hammarskjöld, *Markings*, trans. Leif Sjöberg and W. H. Auden (New York: Knopf, 1964), p. 120 (see also pp. 68ff. and p. 19).

17. Nietzsche, *Thus Spake Zarathustra*, trans. Walter Kaufmann in *The Portable Nietzsche* (New York: Viking, 1954), pp. 434 and 436.

18. Kafka, Aphorism #3 in *The Great Wall of China*, p. 163.

19. Kierkegaard, *The Concept of Dread*, trans. Walter Lowrie (Princeton, N.J.: Princeton University Press, 1957), pp. 38ff.

20. I John 4:18.

21. John 12:27 and 31.

22. John 4:24.

23. John 6:63.

24. John 1:14.

25. See Isak Dinesen, cited in Chapter 1, note 5.

26. John 15:11 (see also 17:13).
27. The title is translated by James Baillie as *The Phenomenology of Mind* (New York: Macmillan, 1961), but the word "spirit" is a more accurate rendering of Hegel's word *Geist*.
28. John 3:8.
29. John 19:9 (my translation) and 13:36.
30. See John 3:3ff.
31. Jean-Paul Sartre, *Being and Nothingness*, trans. Hazel E. Barnes (New York: Washington Square, 1966), p. 754.
32. C. S. Lewis, *Surprised by Joy* (London: Geoffrey Bles, 1955), pp. 23f.
33. Sartre, *The Words*, trans. Bernard Frechtman (New York: Fawcett, 1966), p. 158.
34. See Rilke, cited in Chapter 1, note 8.

CHAPTER 3

1. Laurens van der Post, *The Heart of the Hunter* (London: Penguin, 1965), p. 139.
2. See Nicholas of Cusa, *The Vision of God*, trans. Emma Gurney Salter (New York: Ungar, 1960).
3. Nietzsche, *Thus Spake Zarathustra*, p. 375.
4. Kafka, *The Castle*, trans. Willa and Edwin Muir (New York: Modern Library, 1969), p. 128.
5. Genesis 1:4, 10, 12, 17, 21, 25, 31.
6. Kafka, *The Castle*, p. 219 ("Her gaze was cold, clear, and steady as usual, it was never leveled exactly on the object she was looking at, but in some disturbing way always a little past it, hardly perceptibly, but yet unquestionably past it, not from weakness, apparently, nor from embarrassment, nor from duplicity, but from a persistent and dominating desire for isolation, which she herself perhaps only became conscious of in this way").
7. I Corinthians 13:12 (King James Version). See also Galatians 4:9: ". . . but now that you have come to know God, or rather to be known by God. . . ."
8. Jorge Luis Borges, *Other Inquisitions 1937–1952*, trans. Ruth L. C. Simms (New York: Washington Square, 1966), p. 98.
9. "The name 'solitary' is to be avoided too so as not to take away the companionship of the three persons." Aquinas, *Summa Theologiae*, I, q. 31, a. 2 (my translation). Cf. *ibid.*, a. 3.
10. Matthew 11:27. See also Luke 10:22.
11. *Meister Eckhart*, ed. Franz Pfeiffer, trans. C. de B. Evans (London: John M. Watkins, 1947), p. 59 (from the Sermon "Scio hominem in Christo"). I have modified the translation slightly, mainly "laughs to" instead of "laughs into" and "begets" wherever Eckhart has "birt." Cf. the text in *Deutsche Mystiker*, vol. 2, *Meister Eckhart*, ed. Franz

Pfeiffer (Aalen: Scientia Verlag, 1962) (originally Leipzig, 1857), p. 79.

12. See Anders Nygren, *Agape and Eros*, trans. Philip S. Watson (London: S.P.C.K., 1953). See especially the tabulated points of contrast, p. 210.

13. See Martin Buber, *Hasidism and Modern Man*, ed. and trans. Maurice Friedman (New York: Harper, 1966), p. 207 (also p. 199).

14. *Ibid.*, p. 186.

15. *Ibid.*, pp. 187ff. Spinoza equates the love and the glory ("This love or blessedness is, in the Bible, called Glory"), *Ethics*, V, 36, note (p. 265).

16. Romans 8:15 (King James Version) and Galatians 4:6. See also Mark 14:36, where Jesus uses the name "Abba."

17. John 1:14. See also 17:24 ("to behold my glory").

18. John 17:5.

19. John 17:22 and 1:12. I am thinking here especially of the "I am" statements where there is no predicate, John 8:24, 28, 58. I owe the idea of connecting the "I am" statements with the Shekinah to a conversation with David Daube at Berkeley, California, in 1970.

20. John 1:5 (adapted from the King James Version).

21. Blaise Pascal, *Pensées*, 602, in Pascal, *Oeuvres Completes*, ed. Jacques Chevalier (Paris: Gallimard, Bibliotheque de la Pleiade, 1954), pp. 1280f. (my translation).

CHAPTER 4

1. Loren Eiseley, *The Night Country* (New York: Scribner, 1971), p. 224.

2. Kafka, Aphorism #48 in *The Great Wall of China*, p. 171.

3. C. G. Jung, *Psychology and Alchemy* (London: Routledge and Kegan Paul, 1974), p. 28.

4. Kafka, Aphorism #67, *op. cit.*, p. 175.

5. Martin Lings, *A Sufi Saint of the Twentieth Century* (Berkeley and Los Angeles: University of California Press, 1971), pp. 204f. (I have put together two of his aphorisms here.)

6. Eckhart, *Defensio*, IX, 19, trans. Raymond B. Blakney in *Meister Eckhart* (New York: Harper, 1941), p. 288.

7. "Solus Deus illabitur animae," Aquinas, *Summa Theologiae*, III, q. 64, a. a.

8. Plato, *Apology*, 23A, trans. Benjamin Jowett in *The Dialogues of Plato*, vol. 1 (New York: Random House, 1937), p. 406.

9. Mark 2:7 (King James Version), Luke 5:21.

10. Matthew 7:12 and Luke 11:4 (both in King James Version). See also Hannah Arendt, *The Human Condition* (Garden City, N.Y.: Doubleday, 1959), pp. 212ff., on Jesus and the power to forgive.

11. Genesis 5:22, 24 (Enoch); 6:9 (Noah).

12. Tolstoy, *The Death of Ivan Ilych*, trans. Louise and Aylmer Maude (London: Oxford, 1971), p. 73.

13. See above, note 2.

14. See Herbert Mason's version cited in Chapter 1, note 13. Massignon and Gardet translate "all that matters for the ecstatic is that the Unique should reduce him to Unity" in the article cited in Chapter 1, note 12, p. 101B. That "Unity," however, is the "unity of witness" spoken of below in note 15.

15. "Unity of witness" (*wahdat al-shuhud*), cf. Massignon and Gardet, *op. cit.*, p. 102. Massignon contrasts this with "unity of being" (*wahdat al wudjud*), the term used by Sufi masters starting with Ibn Arabi, e.g., Al-Alawi in Martin Lings, *op. cit.*, pp. 121ff. Instead of reducing "unity of witness" to "unity of being," as Lings suggests, we might consider understanding the "unity of being" as a "unity of witness."

A parallel would be Meister Eckhart, who has it that "Existence is God" ("Esse est Deus") (see Eckhart, *Parisian Questions and Prologues*, trans. Armand A. Maurer [Toronto: Pontifical Institute of Medieval Studies, 1974], pp. 85f. and 93), but who also has it that "The eye with which I see God is the same eye with which God sees me" (see the passage cited above in note 6). Instead of saying my eye and God's eye are one because my existence and God's existence are one, I could say that our existence is one insofar as our knowing and loving are one. There is some hint that Eckhart understood it this way in *Parisian Questions and Prologues*, pp. 43ff, where he is saying "Existence and understanding are the same in God."

16. Spinoza, Letters 39–41 (1666), trans. R. H. M. Elwes, *Chief Works*, vol. 2, pp. 351ff.

17. John 10:30.

18. John 16:32 (see also 8:16).

19. John 17:22f. (see also 17:11, 21).

20. Alfred Adler, *Social Interest: A Challenge to Mankind*, trans. John Linton and Richard Vaughan (New York: Capricorn, 1964), p. 42.

21. Matthew 19:17.

22. W. B. Yeats, *A Vision* (New York: Collier, 1966), p. 119.

CHAPTER 5

1. Marcel Proust, *A la recherche du temps perdu*, vol. 1 (Paris: Gallimard, Bibliothèque de la Pleiade, 1954), p. 100 (my translation).

2. On the distinction between "self" and "soul" see my book, *A Search for God in Time and Memory* (New York: Macmillan, 1969), pp. 172ff.

3. See above, Chapter 1, note 7.

4. W. B. Yeats, *Collected Poems* (New York: Macmillan, 1956), p. 230.

5. Albert Camus, *Exile and Kingdom* (London: Penguin, 1974), p. 25.

6. *Ibid.*, p. 29.

7. John 4:14.

8. John 4:10 (King James Version).

9. John 4:9.
10. John 4:14.
11. Yeats, *A Vision*, p. 180.
12. Jung, *Answer to Job* in *Psychology and Religion: West and East*, trans. R. F. C. Hull (Princeton, N.J.: Princeton University Press, 1969), p. 451.
13. *Ibid.*
14. I John 4:18. Cf. Jung's critique of John and of this very passage, *Answer to Job*, pp. 449ff.; but it seems to me that John is speaking out of an experience of going through fear to love, not simply of repressing fear.
15. Camus, *Exile and Kingdom*, pp. 25f.
16. See Mark Twain (Samuel L. Clemens), *The Autobiography of Mark Twain*, ed. Charles Neider (New York: Harper, 1959), pp. 42f.
17. Camus, *A Happy Death*, trans. Richard Howard (New York: Knopf, 1972), p. 113.
18. Dag Hammarskjöld, *Markings*, p. 97.
19. See his poem "The Dark Night of the Soul," which he comments on in two of his works, *The Ascent of Mount Carmel* and *The Dark Night of the Soul*, both translated by E. Allison Peers (London: Sheed and Ward, 1953). The "night of sense" is described in Book One and the "night of spirit" in Book Two of *The Dark Night of the Soul*.
20. Matthew 4:4.
21. Matthew 26:39 and 27:46.
22. The phrase "happy night" occurs in the third stanza of his poem, cited in note 19, above.
23. Camus, *Exile and Kingdom*, p. 26.
24. Heraclitus, Fragment 62 (my translation) in Hermann Diels, *Fragmente der Vorsokratiker*, fifth edition, vol. 1 (Berlin: Weidmann, 1934), p. 164. See also Fragments 76 and 77, *ibid.*, p. 168.
25. "Incipit vita nova," the motto Dante formulates in the opening sentence of *La Vita Nuova*. Here and throughout I am making my own translations from the edition by Paget Toynbee, *Le opere di Dante Alighieri* (Oxford: Oxford University Press, 1924).
26. See Jung, *Two Essays on Analytical Psychology*, trans R. F. C. Hull (New York: Pantheon, 1953), pp. 186ff.
27. Jung, *Memories, Dreams, Reflections*, trans. Richard and Clara Winston (New York: Vintage, 1963), p. 5.
28. *Loc. cit.* in note 25, above (my translation).
29. Rainer Maria Rilke, *Selected Letters 1902–1926*, trans. R. F. C. Hull (London: Macmillan, 1946), pp. 392f. (Letter to Witold von Hulewicz, Nov. 13, 1925).
30. *Ibid.*
31. Heraclitus, Fragment 60 (my translation) in Diels, *op. cit.*, p. 164.
32. Heraclitus, Fragment 18 (my translation) in Diels, *op. cit.*, p. 155.

CHAPTER 6

1. Henry David Thoreau, *Walden*, ed. J. Lyndon Shanley (Princeton, N.J.: Princeton University Press, 1971), p. 8.
2. Sigmund Freud, *The Interpretation of Dreams*, trans. James Strachey in *The Complete Psychological Works of Sigmund Freud*, vol. 5 (London: Hogarth, 1958), pp. 460ff.
3. Dante, *The Banquet* (*Il Convivio*), II, 16 (Toynbee, p. 270)—"first love"; and III, 1 (Toynbee, p. 271)—"second love."
4. Matthew 10:39. See also Matthew 16:25, Mark 8:35, Luke 9:24 and 14:26, and John 12:25.
5. "I am again myself," Kierkegaard concludes in *Repetition*, trans. Walter Lowrie (New York: Harper, 1964), pp. 125f.
6. Kierkegaard, *The Sickness unto Death*, pp. 147, 182, 262.
7. This is the last line of *The Divine Comedy* (*Paradiso*, XXXIII, 145) (my translation).
8. Yeats, "The Tower" in *Collected Poems*, p. 197.
9. Kierkegaard, *The Sickness unto Death*, p. 146.
10. On the rise of the modern sense of death, see my books, *The City of the Gods* (New York: Macmillan, 1965), pp. 172ff. and 191ff., and *A Search for God in Time and Memory*, pp. 76ff.
11. This is the last stanza of Donne's last poem, "A Hymne to God the Father." See John Donne, *The Divine Poems*, ed. Helen Gardner (Oxford: Clarendon Press, 1959), p. 51.
12. On the two certainties, "I am" and "I will die," see my book, *A Search for God in Time and Memory*, pp. 18f.
13. Descartes uses the formula "I am, I exist" (*Je suis, j'existe*) in his *Meditations*, II, and the formula "I think, therefore I am" (*Je pense, donc je suis*) in his *Discourse on Method*, IV, and in his *Principles of Philosophy*, I, 7. See Descartes, *Oeuvres et lettres*, ed. André Bridoux (Paris: Gallimard, 1952), pp. 147f., 175, and 573.
14. See my book, *The Way of All the Earth* (New York: Macmillan, 1972), p. 180, on the connection between "I am" and the split between mind and body and on the connection between the Buddhist doctrine of "no-self" (*anatta*), that "I am" is an illusion, and the integration of mind and body.
15. Jean Cocteau, *Orpheus*, trans. John Savacool in Cocteau, *The Infernal Machine and Other Plays* (New York: New Directions, 1963), p. 128.
16. Dante, *The Banquet* (*Il Convivio*), II, 7 (Toynbee, p. 159).
17. *Ibid.*, 8 (Toynbee, p. 259).
18. Descartes gives definitions "in geometric fashion" of the three substances in his reply to the second series of objections to his *Meditations*. See Descartes, *Oeuvres et lettres*, p. 391 (Definition VI—Mind, VII—Body, VIII—God).
19. The "four hypostases" are the topics of Plotinus' six *Enneads* (Body or Matter is dealt with in the earlier ones, IV is on Soul, V on Mind, and

VI on God or the One) much as the "three substances" are the topics of Descartes' six *Meditations* (the first two on Mind, the second two on God, and the last two on Body).

There is a turning away from body, it is true, in Plotinus' vision. He envisions an ascending movement in which one leaves one's body behind, rising from body to soul to mind to God. It is like the movement the man we have been imagining has gone through in his journey into solitude. We can envision a descending movement, however, in which one returns to one's body, coming from God to mind to soul to body. That, in fact, is the very movement the man we are imagining is making now in his journey back from solitude to the human circle.

20. Dag Hammarskjöld, *Markings*, p. 82.
21. *Ibid.*, p. 205.
22. Hegel, *The Phenomenology of Mind*, p. 237.
23. "The truth which conscious certainty of self realizes," *ibid.*, p. 218.
24. Nietzsche, *My Sister and I* (New York: Bridgehead Books, 1951), p. 233.

CHAPTER 7

1. William Morris, vol. 2 of *The Well at the World's End* in vol. 19 of *The Collected Works of William Morris* (London: Longmans, 1913), p. 37.
2. *Ibid.*, pp. 81f.
3. John 4:14.
4. See Dante, *Inferno*, I, 2f.
5. See above, Chapter 6, notes 16 and 17.
6. Dante, *Inferno*, I, 76–78 (my translation).
7. John 10:17.
8. John 10:18.
9. John 1:12.
10. See Yeats, *Collected Poems*, pp. 231f., the second half of "A Dialogue of Self and Soul," where the dialogue ceases and "Self" carries on in a monologue.
11. See Nietzsche, *op. cit.*, p. 269, where he imagines the Superman on his deathbed saying, "Was that life? Well then! Once more!"
12. John 11:25.
13. Henrik Ibsen, *When We Dead Awaken*, trans. Michael Meyer (Garden City, N.Y.: Doubleday, 1960), p. 369.
14. Deuteronomy 6:5. See also Matthew 22:37, Mark 12:30, and Luke 10:27. Note how in each of the Gospel passages the phrase is added "and with all your mind."
15. Ibsen, *op. cit.*, pp. 343 and 345.
16. See above, Chapter 6, note 7.
17. Cf. Meyer's translation of the first ending, *ibid.*, p. 318, and of the final ending, *ibid.*, pp. 380f.
18. Ephesians 5:14.

19. John 20:18 and 25, Luke 24:34.
20. Luke 24:32.
21. John 11:25f.
22. Shakespeare, *Richard III*, Act V, scene 3, lines 121ff.
23. *Ibid.*, line 184.
24. *Ibid.*, lines 201f.
25. II Samuel 6:14.
26. See *The Oxford English Dictionary*, vol. 5 (Oxford: Clarendon Press, 1933), p. 161, where "heart and soul" is taken to mean "The whole of one's affections and energies; one's whole being."
27. Yeats, *Collected Poems*, p. 214 (the last line of the poem "Among School Children").
28. Martin Buber, *I and Thou*, second edition, trans. Ronald Gregor Smith (New York: Scribner, 1958), pp. 6, 101 (the eternal "thou" in the human "thou") and p. 63 (the breath of eternal life) ("breath" is also mentioned in the above passages but here it is specified as of "eternal life").
29. Buber, *The Way of Response*, ed. N. N. Glatzer (New York: Schocken, 1966), p. 99.
30. See above, Chapter 5, note 24.
31. John 17:23.
32. This passage is from Kierkegaard, *Repetition*, but instead of Lowrie's translation (p. 125) I am using here Swenson's in his introduction to Kierkegaard, *Philosophical Fragments* (Princeton, N.J.: Princeton University Press, 1962), p. xxix.
33. Buber, *I and Thou*, p. 9.
34. Jorge Luis Borges, "The Meeting in a Dream" in his *Other Inquisitions 1937–1952*, trans. Ruth L. C. Simms (New York: Washington Square, 1966), pp. 101ff.
35. Hegel, *The Phenomenology of Mind*, p. 239 (I have changed the word "bondsman" to "slave").
36. *Ibid.*, p. 237.

CHAPTER 8

1. G. K. Chesterton, *The Man Who Was Thursday* (Harmondsworth, England: Penguin, 1972), p. 61.
2. Rilke, Letter to Princess Marie, December 17, 1912, as translated by J. B. Leishman and Stephen Spender in Rilke, *Duino Elegies* (New York: Norton, 1967), p. 91. See this passage in the full text of letter in *Selected Letters of Rainer Maria Rilke*, trans. R. F. C. Hull (London: Macmillan, 1947), p. 223, and in the original German text in R. M. Rilke and Marie von Thurn und Taxis, *Briefwechsel*, vol. 1 (Zurich: Max Niehans, 1951), p. 248.
3. See Arnold Toynbee, *A Study of History*, vol. 3 (London: Oxford University Press, 1934), pp. 248ff. See my discussions of withdrawal and

return in *The Way of All the Earth*, pp. xff., 14ff., 38ff., 147ff., 165ff., 221ff., and in *Time and Myth*, pp. 100ff.

4. Thoreau, cited above in Chapter 6, note 1.

5. F. L. Woodward, *Some Sayings of the Buddha* (London: Oxford University Press, 1960), p. 11.

6. Isak Dinesen (Karen Blixen), cited above in Chapter 1, note 5.

7. See the examples in Nahum N. Glatzer, *Language of Faith* (New York: Schocken, 1967), especially p. 80 ("The Song of You," where the title is repeated three times at the beginning), also p. 72 (where it is translated "Lord of the Universe"), and p. 241.

8. Kierkegaard, cited above in Chapter 6, note 6.

9. Aquinas speaks of the "pain of sense" (*poena sensus*) and the "pain of loss" (*poena damni*) in his *Summa Contra Gentiles*, IV, 90.

10. Juliana of Norwich, *Revelations of Divine Love*, thirteenth edition, ed. Grace Warrack (London: Methuen, 1949), p. 56.

11. Genesis 3:8.

12. Simone Weil, *Gravity and Grace*, trans. Emma Craufurd (London: Routledge and Kegan Paul, 1952), p. 74.

13. Pascal, *Pensées*, 481 (my translation). The text in *Oeuvres Completes de Pascal*, ed. Jacques Chevalier (Paris: Gallimard, 1954), p. 1222, is "voila ce que c'est que la foi: Dieu sensible au coeur, non a la raison."

14. Ezra Pound, trans., *Confucius* (New York: New Directions, 1951), p. 27.

15. Witter Bynner, trans., *The Way of Life according to Laotzu* (New York: Capricorn, 1944), p. 29.

16. See my discussion of this text in *The Way of All the Earth*, pp. 219ff.

17. See A. Guillaume, *The Life of Muhammad*, a translation of Ibn Ishaz's *Sirat Rasul Allah* (Pakistan: Oxford University Press, 1968), p. 683. I have reworded the translation, substituting "living and undying" for "alive, immortal."

Index

Index

[167]